VOICES

& VISIONS

VOICES & VISIONS

REFIGURING ETHNOGRAPHY IN COMPOSITION

EDITED BY

**CRISTINA KIRKLIGHTER
CLOE VINCENT
JOSEPH M. MOXLEY**

Boynton/Cook
HEINEMANN
Portsmouth, NH

Boynton/Cook Publishers, Inc.
A subsidiary of Reed Elsevier Inc.
361 Hanover Street
Portsmouth, NH 03801-3912

Offices and agents throughout the world

Library of Congress Cataloging-in-Publication Data

Voices and visions: refiguring ethnography in composition/edited by Cristina Kirklighter,
    Cloe Vincent, Joe Moxley.
        p.   cm.
    Includes bibliographical references.
    ISBN 0-86709-435-4
    1. Ethnology—Authorship.   2. Ethnology—Field work.
3. Communication in ethnology.   I. Kirklighter, Cristina.
II. Vincent, Cloe.   III. Moxley, Joe.
GN307.7.V65   1997   97-28100
305.8'001—dc21   CIP

Editor: Peter R. Stillman
Cover design: Darci Mehall
Manufacturing: Louise Richardson

Printed in the United States of America on acid-free paper
01 00 99 98 97 DA 1 2 3 4 5 6 7 8 9

Contents

Introduction

> For writing researchers . . . ethnography seems both puzzling and enchanting—puzzling because its methodology is difficult to standardize and enchanting because the profession has sensed ethnography's potential for delivering new kinds of data and for providing answers that are otherwise elusive.
>
> —Ralph Cintron, "Wearing a Pith Helmet at a Sly Angle"

Over the past ten to fifteen years, compositionists have been analyzing the rationale behind all research methodologies more closely than ever. Researchers have questioned the ethics, procedures, and authority of ethnographic modes of inquiry. In this anthology, we bring together diverse yet interrelated chapters that address some of the puzzles and potential enchantments of ethnography for literacy and writing researchers. Contributors add to, recapitulate, and extend conversations about the ethical and practical challenges ethnography researchers face—from defense of ethnographic methodology and ethnographic reports as a developing genre in literacy research to discoveries of the new and rich perspectives ethnography highlights. We scrutinize, for example, the situation of researchers and those they observe, as well as how narratives both usefully refigure but also problematize data.

As ethnographers who strive to make contributions to our expanding field, we look not just at ethnographic but also at quasi-ethnographic (or perhaps postethnographic) research. For example, ethnographies may be considered *quasi* or *micro* ethnographies if they involve less than a year of research in the field (often only a semester, for example). On the other hand, ethnographies in which the authorial *I* is used and in which personal experience is emphasized, like those of Wendy Bishop, Mike Rose, and many others, could be called postmodern ethnographies or autoethnographies because their style is less formal and more confessional than ethnographies written in the nineteenth and early twentieth centuries. Within our field, some rely on the precepts of logical positivism and employ social-science terms, whereas others assert that ethnographers should valorize phenomenological principles and apply the tactics of narrative thinking. Supplanting *objectivity* with *intersubjectivity* is also a critical issue for both cultural anthropologists and compositionists. For the most part, the actual ethnographic research conducted to date in composition studies is significantly different from the traditionally positivistic and strictly empirical research first introduced by anthropologists. The research in composition studies is often (and perhaps necessarily) less comprehensive with, for example, fewer researchers spending less time in the *field*. It is also, however, like much of the current research in anthropology and sociology, usually based on social epistemic and postpositivistic rather than positivistic assumptions about human behavior and potential. Our use of different methodologies reflects compositionists' situatedness within a multivoiced and postmodern world.

In *The Making of Knowledge in Composition* (1987), Stephen North reported that only 2000 pages of books, dissertations, articles, and papers on the subject of ethnography had been published in composition. Since then—despite North's prediction that ethnography would fall into disuse and disfavor— ethnography has increasingly become the methodology of choice. Our research (through ERIC and MLA) indicates a rapid increase to at least 5300 pages between 1987 and 1995. Additionally, since 1990, nine of the twelve winning studies of The Promising Researcher Award (established in 1970 by the NCTE Committee) were either ethnographies or they incorporated qualitative methods in their designs. The winning studies represent a gradual shift from transitional designs combining ethnographic methods with quantitative techniques to contextualized, descriptive, and interpretative ethnographies. All three of the 1994 winners are ethnographies (Sarbo, 1996, 81).

As we can see, ethnographic inquiry has played an increasingly prominent role in composition studies. This book examines the ways ethnographic and quasi-ethnographic research is used by researchers in composition studies, cultural studies, and English education. It is written for the many researchers conducting ethnographic research and for graduate professors who are chairing dissertations that employ ethnographic methods.

Today's teachers use qualitative methods to investigate their classrooms, thanks in part to the teacher-researcher movement, the National Writing Project, the emergence of literacy issues, and the examples of Atwell, Brooke, Bishop, Calkins, Cross, Graves, Heath, Sunstein, and others. We tackle the different issues and questions today's ethnographers face:

1. What is unique about how compositionists conduct ethnography?

2. Should positivism or postpositivism inform the authority of ethnography?

3. To what extent should ethnographies be about the ethnographer, the research community, or the surrounding community?

4. To what extent should an ethnographer act as a cultural worker or an objective scientist?

5. How can ethnographers "tell the truth" when doing so reflects negatively on the communities or when they cannot get respondents' written permission to be published?

As we explore diverse theoretical, ethical, and pedagogical concerns, contributors do the following: debate some of the ongoing conversations about this methodology and explore how ethnographic methods help us to understand further the effects of race, gender, and class in learning styles, literacy, and communication dynamics. Although some chapters are themselves miniethnographies, every chapter focuses self-reflexively on exploring how writing and literacy specialists use ethnographic approaches to research. We respond to the need for contextualized research, learning from the first-hand experiences of each other and of colleagues in anthropology and sociology. Both established and emerging scholars grapple with the dissertation process, as well as their concerns about protecting anonymity and writing authoritative reports. Focusing on the practical and philosophical challenges this methodology introduces, contributors refigure the academic article genre and reexamine what makes the methodology authoritative and useful in general.

In the first chapter, "North Northwest: Ethnography and The Making of Knowledge in Composition," Eric Branscomb describes why compositionists have turned to ethnographic research. He explains,

> Two philosophical and cultural forces, certainly not new in 1987 nor unknown, have begun increasingly to shape our profession: feminism and postmodernism. And both of these forces seem to be directing composition studies away from paradigmatic models [, focusing on theory-making and taxonomies] and toward narrative models, of which Ethnography is a prime.

Branscomb describes ways the mix and match of methodologies that Stephen North saw as an ethnographic crutch could arguably be seen as a vital support for the interdisciplinary, postmodern, and feminist turn that has permeated every facet of composition since its inception.

The next section of the anthology, "Authority and the Rhetoric of Ethnography," addresses another key concern for ethnographers: methodological authority. Robert Brooke, Keith Rhodes, and Kristi Yager provide analysis of what makes ethnographic inquiry valuable and authoritative. As North explains, "among users and consumers alike, [there is] considerable confusion about what sort of authority [ethnography] has" (313). Consequently, there are often reservations about publishing ethnographic work. Out of this confusion, however, ethnographic research has the potential to dramatically refigure issues about how authority is analyzed and assessed in the first place. For example, greater acceptance of both the authority of first-hand experience and of collaboratively written reports will help in overcoming many obstacles. As a research methodology, ethnography frequently emphasizes shared authority, just as collaborative writing (and classrooms) do. It supplants a generally hierarchical model with a more interactive and organic one. Unlike the positivistic assumption that people and texts should strive for a single, best answer to problems and assessments of situations, phenomenological ethnographic research stresses allowing for multiple perspectives, solutions, and assessments.

Robert Brooke demonstrates the importance of this shared authority by revisiting a previous work: his critically acclaimed "Underlife and Writing Instruction," which won the Braddock Award in 1988. As he reviews his observation notebook, reflective writing, and article draft for "Underlife and Writing Instruction," he sees the ethnographic process as grounded in rhetorical invention. Just as rhetoricians may employ invention heuristics, so too must the ethnographer follow certain exploratory methodologies prior to writing up an ethnography. Brooke points out that what one chooses to explore is selective. His interest in Erving Goffman's underlife, along with his readings in anthropology, philosophy, and developmental psychology, all contributed to his focus while he was observing a classroom. Brooke eloquently explains that foregrounding the rhetorical forces that shape our ethnographies makes us more critical of how we represent ourselves, as well as others, within our studies.

In the next chapter, "Ethnography or Psychography," Keith Rhodes also examines how language and conventions affect the authority of ethnographic and quasi-ethnographic writing. He finds the word *ethnography* inadequate to name a mode of inquiry that, over the years, has developed into a study of ethics and culture. Rhodes believes we are not studying whole cultures in the classroom, but rather conducting *psychography*: "thickly described writing exploring the connections of individual psyches with specific cultural conditions." We, as compositionists, have no hope of completely capturing a classroom culture (or even a subculture of a classroom), nor should we pretend to if we want to be ethically responsible.

In Kristi Yager's chapter, "Composition's Appropriation of Ethnographic Authority," she critiques composition ethnographers for portraying themselves as teacher-heroes. Yager claims that many of these introductory personal narratives serve as a rhetorical device to bond with other teachers and then quickly vanish into a sea of objective pronouncements about the students or culture under study. These ethnographers move from a seemingly phenomenological epistemology to a text grounded in "a positivistic, empirical tradition." Adopting a critical anthropological approach is one way to overcome reverting to the traditional assertion of authority within one's own narrative. As Yager explains, "Critical anthropologists examine the discursive elements of ethnographic methodology in order to discover the underlying assumptions of a given ethnographer's work. . . . [They] seek to uncover the power-knowledge relationships which structure and determine a given author's meaning."

In the third section, "The Ethics of Anonymity," three writers examine the challenges and compromises ethnographers face while protecting the identities of people they observe. In their chapter "Covering One's Tracks: Respecting and Preserving Informant Anonymity," John Lofty and Richard Blot use a series of arguments and counterarguments to examine the complexities involved in fully addressing the issue of anonymity in ethnographic reports. Lofty reflects on his experiences trying to maintain anonymity for an ethnographic study of students in a fishing community on a Maine-island. For

Lofty, preserving anonymity helps to ensure the psychological well-being of participants, the trust between the researchers and participants, and the freedom to report both positive and negative findings. As a cultural anthropologist, Blot responds to Lofty by interpreting the American Anthropological Association's *Statements on Ethics*. He counterargues Lofty's position, questioning whether one can keep a setting, and participants anonymous and still depict the factual nature of the description. Does this anonymity render these subjects as objects? Does it free researchers, but make the subjects powerless to control representations? How can we know which voices are represented? This chapter helps readers assess the pros and cons of anonymity that they may encounter in their own studies.

Further demonstrating some of the ethical—and arguably postmodern—conundrums faced by researchers, Gwen Gorzelsky uses both Marxist and literary theorists in her chapter "Materialist Methods: Ethnography and Transformation." She describes the problems she confronted while trying to capture individual representations of disenfranchised nonacademic subjects. Her use of materialist dialectics is grounded in theories by Marx, Louis Althusser, and Richard Johnson, as well as her discussion of literary theorists like George Marcus, Barbara Myerhoff, Jay Ruby, Paul Rabinow, and Gayatri Spivak. Gorzelsky helps composition ethnographers see the important role interdisciplinary theories play in tackling the "tensions of representation." By offering us an ethnographic form and practice that acknowledges the (im)possibility of representing others (and their conceptual frames), Gorzelsky still struggles to enact admittedly limited, problematic representations to make her own framework more concrete and complex. Through a revision of ethnographic practice and its developing conceptual frameworks, Gorzelsky hopes we find a better balance of power between academics and community workers within literacy project environments.

In the fourth section, "Cultural and Political Perspectives," writers look at collaborative-learning cultures from a variety of angles. Geoffrey Cross, in "Writing Through the Grapevine: The Influence of Social Network Clusters on Team-Written Texts," acknowledges the necessity of revising conceptual frameworks about group formation, turning to the area of network analysis as a vehicle for probing *submerged* and *subcultural* networks of communication. An analysis of these network social structures (groups, group linkers, dyads, and isolates) employs both quantitative and qualitative methods. Cross provides important applications for composition ethnographers who—especially early in their fieldwork—need both to gather data and excavate the subculture of collaborative-writing webs. Network analysis provides ethnographers with ways to address many contemporary academic issues, such as power, generative ability (e.g., distinctions between isolates and dyads), style, interorganizational influence, gender, and technology.

Moving between outsider and insider perspectives, Ruoyi Wu, in her chapter "Writing Bio(Life) into Ethnography," questions whether the words *ethno* (other people) and *graphy* (writing) really capture the current shift toward ethnobiography: "writing that includes the historical contexts of both the researcher and the researched." Wu's blurring of distinctions between ethnography and other areas of study, such as autobiography, biography, history, and literary criticism, reflects her desire, as a Chinese and feminist woman, to stretch ethnography's definition for cultural reasons. For her, Western polarities—between the subjective and objective, the emotional and rational, the personal and social, and the insider and outsider—represent social constructs that do not meet with her cultural perceptions about how to conduct ethnography. Wu's renaming of ethnography allows compositionists grounded in Western discourse to view this field from an Eastern perspective.

In the next chapter, Kay Losey describes how ethnographies can create students as heroes and teachers as villains by predominantly focusing on the student culture while ignoring the teacher's perspective. Ethnographers studying the classroom must include a *macroethnographic* dimension to educational *microethnography* to achieve greater insight, embracing the realization that all perspectives in this community are interpreted by the ethnographer herself. In ethnographic academic discourse, ethnographers need to move away from research that leads to simple conclusions and toward an approach that embraces the multiple communities in the classroom.

Marcy Taylor examines authority and cultural issues of institutionally bound rituals among students and teachers. She explores how our interpretations of successful or unsuccessful writing conferences significantly rely on our conditioned perceptions. Successful writing conference dialogue (a trope of literacy) is often measured by the amount of free discussion between teacher and student. This is usually interpreted as the empowered student taking action. Students entering the conference for specific information to improve their grade (i.e., "tell me what you want") are considered unsuccessful. When Taylor begins to study her students' perceptions of conference goals (their rituals of schooling), however, she sees that their approaches are one way to manage ambiguity between teacher and student cultures. By revisiting a conference with one of her own students, Taylor reinterprets her fieldwork in light of the disjuncture between cultures and urges ethnographers to further examine these unfamiliar tropes.

The final section of the book, "Doing Fieldwork as Graduate Students and Faculty Members," provides guidance and advice to new ethnographers. Wendy Bishop reflects on lessons learned from her first major ethnography to her second. While doing her first ethnography as a graduate student, Bishop pushed forward in her ethnographic research and writing to meet an extrinsic goal of completing her dissertation and locating a job. The second ethnographic project, conducted as a professor, is not yet completed. In her second ethnography, she admits to missing distinctions between the first and second groups studied, falling into a technician's pattern, and becoming distracted with writing essays about ethnography. However, instead of viewing this second project as incomplete and a failure, Bishop sees it as a learning process. As a prolific writer and a professor immersed in teaching classes about research methods and current poststructural discussions, she has come to realize that the ethnographic life entails an existence without boundaries between writing up and writing about ethnographies. Through her self-reflective tale, Bishop ends by providing ideas about where the second ethnography and beyond takes us in relation to intrinsic and extrinsic goals, to research authority issues, and, finally, to living (and enjoying) the ethnographic life.

In the final chapter,"Ethnographic Dissertations: Avoiding the Traps," Mara Casey, Kate Garretson, Carol Peterson Haviland, and Neal Lerner self-reflexively examine how the ethnographic dissertation process challenges both faculty members and graduate students. Through their collaboratively written chapter, readers begin to see that more successful director-graduate student relationships mirror, in some ways, current ethnographic epistemology. For example, they point out how successful relationships focus on careful readings of participant language and texts and on participatory story-making; they rely on collaborative inquiry, on multiple perspectives, and on honoring the local as well as the global. Through their experiences as graduate students and faculty members, these four writers demonstrate collaboration in action. They also show how collaborative, self-reflexive writing about ethnographic dissertations paves the way to refigure the traditional dissertation process.

This collection is directed to all writing specialists who view their classrooms and other teaching sites as places where valuable research takes place. Because of space limitations, our aim is to introduce and problematize writing specialists' use of ethnography. Providing conclusive viewpoints about this methodology's potential, or what Gesa Kirsch and Patricia Sullivan call *methodological consensus,* is beyond the scope of our book (10). While focusing only on ethnographic inquiry, we, like Kirsch and Sullivan, also "see the methods and issues covered in each part as more fluid and interactive than the visual and physical divisions suggest" (5). We hope that the anthology, as a whole, will encourage grouping and regrouping of ideas contained in individual pieces and musing(s) about multiple conclusions along many paths. We hope our voices and visions will give future researchers both direction and inspiration.

1

North Northwest:
Ethnography and The Making of Knowledge in Composition[1]

H. Eric Branscomb

"This is not necessarily going to be a popular book." (1989)
James Raymond

"I am but mad north-north-west; when the wind is southerly I know
a hawk from a handsaw."

Hamlet, II.ii.356

It has been nearly ten years since Stephen North (1987) published *The Making of Knowledge in Composition: Portrait of an Emerging Field.* For North, writing in the mid-1980s, *Composition* had emerged[2] as a professional field just two decades earlier, and its survival was already in question. With a diverse heritage of seemingly incompatible progenitors (which to others in the field, such as Janet Emig, was evidence of an invigorating "tacit tradition") and internal squabbling among the various camps of scholars, researchers, and practitioners, it seemed to North that Composition would destroy itself and that its remaining parts would be reabsorbed into their constituent fields: linguistics, psychology, literary criticism, among others. He writes,

> It might not be too much to claim, in fact, that for all the rhetoric about unity
> in pursuit of one or another goal, Composition as a knowledge-making
> society is gradually pulling itself apart. Not branching out or expanding,
> although these might be politically more palatable descriptions, but

> fragmenting: gathering into communities or clusters of communities among
> which relations are becoming increasingly tenuous (364).

And he concludes,

> It is not difficult to envision what will happen if, as is most likely, these
> forces continue to operate unopposed in Composition. Quite simply, the
> field, however flimsily coherent now, will lose any autonomous identity
> altogether. Each of its constituent communities will be absorbed by some
> other field with a compatible methodology. (365)

He is especially pessimistic about the impact that Ethnography will have
upon Composition studies. Though he doesn't reserve his overall pessimism
strictly for Ethnography,[3] he does conclude his chapter on "Ethnographers"
with "For all its promise, then, the future of the embattled Ethnographic
community cannot be all that bright" (313). [4]

The Controversy

Owing to its downbeat tone, when *The Making of Knowledge in Composition*
was first published, it was almost immediately controversial. One colleague
told me, in all seriousness, that upon reaching the final page, she put down the
book and seriously considered quitting teaching. The book was undeniably on
everybody's mind in the months following its publication, yet reviews were
usually lukewarm, often hostile. Only Scott Heller (1988) (note: an outsider to
the discipline of Composition), writing for the *Chronicle of Higher Education*
and reporting on the 1988 CCCC, at which point North's book was the hot
topic, finds the book unreservedly praiseworthy; yet even he notes it is
"controversial" (A5). William Irmscher (1988), in *The Harvard Education
Review*, while admitting "it is a good book" (513) and "North's defense of
practitioners . . . is refreshing" (515), complains that it is too long (513), "his
[North's] categories don't work" (514), and that "his work seems to provoke
divisiveness rather than to promote the coherence that dialectic should seek"
(515). He ends with "North calls for an 'intermethodological coherence,' but
he does little to promote it" (516). Elizabeth Rankin (1990) has "a generally
positive reaction" (261), but ultimately argues with North over the "claim to
'private knowledge'" and its "inconsisten[cy] with recent theory" (262).
College Composition and Communication devoted three separate reviews to it:
James Raymond's (1989) mostly positive one ("superb" and "indispensable"
[93] but "reductive" [93] and "fail[s] . . . to come to grips with . . . current
theoretical scholarship" [94]); Richard Lloyd-Jones' (1989) bemused and
uncritical one ("thoughtful, challenging, useful" [1989, 98] and "I think
probably I have not disagreed with North" [99]); and an especially harsh
review—one might also call it an attack—by Richard Larson (1989).

Larson's review and that of David Bartholomae (1988) in *Rhetoric Review*
constituted the harshest of the harsh—in fact, Bartholomae's provoked a

response from North that initiated an exchange of personal letters and a public exchange in the pages of *Rhetoric Review* that at times devolved into sarcasm and name-calling. Larson begins with the obligatory praise: the book, "based . . . on broad and thoughtful reading, has unquestionable value" (95). Then he continues, "The scrutiny of individual writers is witheringly intense." So devastating to individual scholars and writers is North's book, asserts Larson, that it "stands as a warning to writers and directors of dissertations" (96). Of North's criticism of the work of Flower and Hayes, Larson writes, "A reader may be forgiven for doubting the fairness of this evaluative gambit" (96). And finally, "As troubling as North's evaluative procedures is his tone . . . . caustic edge . . . demeaning metaphors . . . North is not content with analyses of the substance of others' writings, he has to derogate, collectively and with little supporting evidence, their motives and attitudes" (97).

Bartholomae first sarcastically parodies the book as a growth-of-a-young man journeying to wisdom, as in *Joseph Andrews*, complains about its "predictable metaphors," its "tired and corrupt 'anthropological' way of speaking" (225). Then he cuts to the quick: "This is the imperialist's representation of the native, and it is odious and, as always, untrue. It undermines the argument of the text..." (225). The book's fairness or objectivity is merely a "guise" (226) and North's assertion of the limitations of research a "bogus surprise" (226). North's logic is "paranoid"; he is ultimately "unable to answer our most pressing questions..." (228). Whence followed the particularly nasty exchange of letters and articles in *Pre/Text*, about which, as they say, the less said, the better.

To listen to the early reviewers, it would seem the profession has a madman in its midst. But is North, in *The Making of Knowledge in Composition*, like Hamlet, merely mad north northwest?

Lore, Practitioner Inquiry, and Ethnography

Much of the controversy surrounding *The Making of Knowledge* sprang from North's use of the word *lore* to characterize the body of knowledge that arises from practitioner inquiry. Aware of its potentially negative, unscholarly, unprofessional connotations, North attempts to valorize or at least neutralize it:

> For some readers, perhaps, the term "lore" will have negative, even denigrative connotations. Lore is what witches know, or herbal healers, or wizards in fantasy fiction. . . . Composition's lore is a body of knowledge very much like those accumulated among practitioners of other arts—art here being broadly conceived—like painting or parenting, to offer an unlikely pair. . . . For example, analyses of ocular function can help inform us about how we "see" paintings, but they cannot tell a Picasso what to do with his brush . . . . (23)

North's protestations about the legitimacy of "lore," however, and his explicit intentions in using the word were apparently not persuasive. Rankin claims parenthetically that North's use of "lore" is accompanied by "an unconvincing disclaimer of its condescending connotations" (262).

But if North's use of the term is taken at face value, we may question what difference exists between "lore" and "practitioner inquiry," if any; and from our 1997 perspective, we may ask how do either of them differ from Ethnography in Composition, if at all?

For North, lore is "the accumulated body of traditions, practices, and beliefs in terms of which Practitioners understand how writing is done, learned, and taught" (22). It has three "functional properties": "anything can become a part of lore," "nothing can ever be dropped from it," and "contributions to it have to be framed in practical terms" (24–25).

Two related issues immediately arise from this description of lore. First, how does one discriminate among various items of lore, among stories which may often contradict each other? By which criteria do we decide what is "good lore" and what is "bad"? Do these terms even have any usefulness? And second, how does lore (Practitioner Knowledge) relate to Practitioner Inquiry?

To answer the first, North refuses to make the distinction at all. *Lore* is lore, he seems to say, a messy conglomeration of often-contradictory stories and pronouncements, which simply is. In the assertion that most rankled Bartholomae ("A Reply"), moreover, North states that the decision to accept and use or reject and discard any specific item of lore is a personal, not a communal, choice. In some ways, as most reviewers noted, this assertion is at best unaware of recent movements in Composition toward a Derridian, Foucaultian postmodern perspective on individual authority and agency (or, to be more precise, the impossibility of it), and, at worst, simply unsatisfying. But Patricia Harkin (1991) has perhaps salvaged *lore* by seeing it, in its acceptance of contradiction, as "antiessentialist" and therefore "postdisciplinary" (134), answering the critics who see *The Making of Knowledge* as unaware of postmodern epistemology.

For North, Practice and Ethnography are separate knowledge bases, lore and Practitioner Inquiry being dealt with in chapter 2 and Ethnography in chapter 9. In fact, Practitioner Inquiry has its own section (Section II: The Practitioners), whereas The Ethnographers chapter is just one subsection of Section IV: The Researchers. And of Practitioners, "less than ten percent" (34) of their work actually qualifies as inquiry, that is, an identifiable contribution to knowledge.

North outlines the steps by which Practice may become formalized as Inquiry, with clear warnings against misconstruction of his "abstraction" as a "lock-step formula":

1. Identifying a Problem
2. Searching for Cause(s)
3. Searching for Possible Solutions
4. Testing Solution in Practice

5. Validation

6. Dissemination (36)

This abstraction sounds very much like scientific method—the formal steps of positivism: the hypothesis generating and hypothesis testing by which the scientific community operates. Jerome Bruner (1986) makes a distinction between two parallel (though ultimately irreducible to one another) ways of knowing: what he calls "paradigmatic thinking" and "narrative thinking" (11–12). Positivist research methodologies rely on paradigmatic thinking. "Physics," for example, "must eventuate in predicting something that is testably right," notes Bruner (14). Even though North acknowledges the looseness of the "Validation" step for practitioner inquiry, he still concludes "either the solution works, in which case the inquirer goes on to identify a new problem; or it doesn't, in which case the investigation recycles" (51). This seems to restrict practitioner inquiry to the paradigmatic mode.

But is practitioner inquiry using Bruner's narrative mode equally possible? Given the developments in Composition over the last ten years, it would seem so.

Consider Bonnie Sunstein's *Composing a Culture: Inside a Summer Writing Program with High School Teachers* (1994). Though not pure narrative and not pure narrative thinking, *Composing a Culture* exemplifies the narratological approach to knowledge-making that is the staple of ethnography, with narrative and thick description predominating and abstraction and generalization interspersed carefully. *Composing a Culture* is an ethnographic study of one summer in the New Hampshire Writing Program, concentrating on three (out of 233) participants. Sunstein is a registered participant in the program she is observing, and she lives on site, mingles freely with the participants, and engages the participants on a number of levels that no traditional positivistic observer or researcher should ever engage in, "shar[ing] food, drink, dorm woes, and writing" (97). It is fair to say her role is one of participant-researcher.

Composing a Culture consists of five chapters (one for each of the three participants' stories, introductory and concluding chapters), a formal afterward, and various appendices. The five chapters are interrupted by five brief "intertexts," similar to the "interludes" of Peter Elbow's *What is English?* (1990). These intertexts serve to present with little explicit commentary brief snapshots of events of the summer that do not fit narratologically with the movement of the main text but do serve to illustrate continuing thematic concerns. Sometimes they work by simple juxtaposition; at others, like quick cuts in a music video, they work to disrupt the too easy coherence, jarring a reader into sudden awareness of multiple perspectives and multiple threads to the stories.

The chapters and the intertexts consist primarily of narratives and thick descriptions. Of one participant/subject, Sunstein writes

> I notice Therese Deni in the circle. She is squirming like a student, nervous. Her brown eyes, large and terrified, follow each speaker around the room. She looks down occasionally, clasped hands covering her mouth and nose. Her head moves slowly from side to side, and her dark hair moves with it; tiny white earrings peek out from under the curls. She is wearing a pink cotton top and crisp white shorts. She crosses her feet at the ankles; her pink socks are cuffed like a little girl's. Her long, sinewy legs seem out of place. When it is her turn she introduces herself, a teacher from California, entering her second year in a very traditional high school. "I don't know how to teach. I am frustrated. I want to convey my love of literature to them, and I don't know how."
>
> Terry acknowledges Therese's dilemma, and explains that she will spend time talking about "how to give up control in the classroom so you can gain it." She confesses to the class, "I controlled because I lacked control." Therese writes rapidly in her notebook. (63)

Structurally, this kind of Ethnographic epistemology bears striking similarities to "teacher lore," emphasizing as it does particularized narratives, the situatedness of the reporter, and the actual construction (rather than discovery) of meaning. In some ways, Ethnography such as Sunstein's is teacher lore with a vengeance, radical teacher lore that both buttresses current lore and critiques it—unpacks it, exposes it in all its details for close examination. And Practitioners such as Sunstein, generating and refining and transmitting lore, shade over into and become indistinguishable from Ethnographers.

Ethnography and Practitioner Inquiry

Two philosophical and cultural forces, certainly neither new nor unknown in 1987, have begun increasingly to shape our profession: feminism and postmodernism. Both of these forces, moreover, seem to be directing Composition studies away from paradigmatic models and toward narrative models, of which Ethnography is a prime example.

Much of the excellent ethnographic research in Composition and literacy studies today is being carried out not by trained anthropologists such as Geertz, but by teacher researchers such as Nancie Atwell, Elizabeth Chiseri-Strater, Lorrie Neilsen, and Bonnie Sunstein. The feminist roots of what I elsewhere have called the *New Epistemologies* (the congruencies of practitioner research, qualitative methodologies, and the radically different ways of knowing engendered by them) (Branscomb, 1995) have been well documented by Ruth Ray (1993), among others. Ray writes,

> For me, the feminist agenda directly parallels the teacher-research agenda: teacher-research approaches composition with a primary concern for the nature of teachers' and students' experiences; it seeks to end the subordination of teachers to researchers; and it attempts to end the domination of theory over practice. In the process, teacher-research, too,

focuses on particularities and differences in the ways that teaching and learning should transpire. (27)

Second, the new polyvocality—the empowerment of those formerly silenced, in our case, the practitioners—allows teachers to tell their own stories, even though they are not university researchers trained in positivist methodologies. Ethnography demands what practitioner-researchers-to-be already have to offer: an immersion in the research site. They do not need to write huge, arcane grants for specialized laboratory research: they have their own classrooms.

This polyvocality is one characteristic of postmodernism, whose manifestations in the Composition field have been called *postdisciplinary* by Patricia Harkin. "[T]eaching itself makes knowledge in ways that are different from, but not less valuable than, the methods of science," she writes. The way in which it makes its knowledge is what North calls *lore*. Lore is "actually defined by its inattention to disciplinary procedures" and "practitioners rarely attend to the theoretical implications of their practice" (125). She concludes that "lore seems (at least potentially) postdisciplinary. In their eclectic foraging among theories, practitioners are antiessentialist as they deal with situations in which single causes cannot be stipulated, in which causes cannot be discriminated from effects. Because it admits contradiction, lore, perhaps unintentionally but nonetheless effectively, can cope with overdetermination" (134).

The Future of Ethnography and Practitioner Inquiry

How accurate has been his prediction of the future of ethnographic studies in Composition? Will Composition and Ethnography survive? Ethnography, as the newest kid on the Composition block, is the last of the categories of knowledge-making that North identifies in *The Making of Knowledge in Composition.* He understands that "the aim of Ethnographic inquiry . . . is to enlarge the 'universe of human discourse,' in Geertz's phrase—not to describe it, or to account for it, or to codify it, but to *enlarge* it, make it bigger" (284). Yet it is this radically different aim that distinguishes ethnographic research from other kinds of research, particularly positivistic modes of controlled experimentation, and that, to North, ultimately presents serious challenges to its survival as a mode of inquiry. First, it is incompatible with positivism: no middle ground or all-encompassing super theory seems possible to North. "It [Ethnography] will not mix and match" (313), he asserts; when trying to visualize the application of positivistic controls to ethnographic methodologies, he concludes "a greater danger still may well lie . . . with the urge for tightness, control" (306).

Second, Ethnography, with its emphasis on the thick descriptions of the here and now, creates "fictions," which "have their limits as knowledge. One such limit lies in the insularity of investigations: the difficulty of somehow extending the findings of an investigation in any one community to any other"

(278). This is the standard charge of "lack of generalizability" that is leveled against ethnographic study: in a critique tantalizingly entitled *What's Wrong with Ethnography?*, Martin Hammersley (1992) concludes, "In summary, there are serious problems with arguments for the general relevance of ethnographic studies" (92). This issue is a serious one for qualitative researchers, not simply because it is at the seat of the methodological and epistemological gulf between qualitative research and positivistic research (and the "positivist culture's latent hostility" [North, 1987, 313]), but also because it asks fundamental questions about the value of ethnographic research to the human race.

Sunstein, writing specifically of the stories told at the summer writing program which was the site of her study but, in effect, noting the value of storytelling for all of us, writes

> The stories in summer fell into very different categories: personal school failures, personal writing failures, teaching failures, classroom bumbling. . . . But as they shared stories, asked questions, and began to disrupt their own views of schooling, the teachers in summer formed a temporary version of what Jerome Bruner calls "folk psychology," which "summarizes not simply how things are but (often implicitly) how they should be (1990 [*sic*], 40)." (1994, 232)

And later, she explains, "Teachers can tell the stories here that they can't tell in a school culture that oppresses them" (233). So the first value of ethnographic stories, which applies to all lore but particularly those stories that have been transmuted into Ethnography by engaged observation and careful writing, is to the individual teacher-researcher-writer. We like (we need!) to tell our stories; it is in a way therapeutic. North (1987), writing of Ethnographers (but without applying it to the Practitioner Researchers who would later use ethnographic methodologies), explains " . . . the process by which they look for themes in their data. They sort, they sift, they work inductively, looking for patterns to 'emerge' from the data. This is so because the process they describe, finally, is the reformation of their own consciousness" (305). "It is," he concludes, "essentially internal, finally accessible only to the individual researcher and, for all its apparent vulnerability, the key link between the investigator and the social discourse from which Ethnographic inquiry derives its power" (306).

Near the end of *The Making of Knowledge*, which North himself characterizes as "gloomy" (375), he warily suggests an alternative scenario for the salvation of Composition: "Three conditions, I think, would have to be met. First, there would have to be heightened methodological consciousness. ...Second, there would have to be a spirit of methodological egalitarianism. ...Third, it would require the re-establishment of Practice as inquiry." (370–371)

The first, I will simply assert, I believe is happening. The second, I suspect is happening more slowly, with strong encampments of enmity dug in (North's phrase "latent hostility" characterizing the current relationship of the positivists and the qualitative researchers is, if anything, unduly charitable). The third condition I want to discuss. The development of Composition has followed a course that North, perhaps over-cautiously, did not anticipate (and probably could not have anticipated): teacher-research has indeed flourished, and it has carried along in its coattails Ethnography. Ruth Ray has noted, "Current scholarship in ethnography, *which informs much teacher research*, supports [the] claim that presenting the particular, in the form of protracted descriptions which emphasize local detail, is important to the making of knowledge" (41, my italics). Ethnography, either pure or in some amalgamated version, is very congenial to practitioner researchers. (In a graduate Composition Research course I taught in the spring of 1994, I covered all modes of research, yet when the final projects from the class came in, all but one student chose ethnography as her primary mode of research).

What has happened in the intervening years between the appearance of *The Making of Knowledge in Composition* and the present is the proliferation of voices of teachers sharing their lore (as North foreshadowed; in fact, as he called for), derived through ethnographic methods (as North did *not* anticipate), sometimes even mixed and matched with case studies, experimental designs, and discourse analysis (Ray, 1993, 93)—the beginnings, at least, of a methodological egalitarianism. Ethnography, surprisingly, has overlaid teacher lore, providing it with an established system of meaning-making and therefore legitimizing it as epistemologically sound. Ethnography infuses lore with a research methodology and thus transmutes lore into knowledge.

This new union of Practitioner Inquiry and Ethnographic methodologies has not, therefore, replaced (and perhaps cannot and perhaps even *should not* replace) positivism as the single mode of knowledge making in Composition. It does exist side by side with positivism, contraries embraced, in a vast democracy of competing voices sharing their own particularized narratives. North's vision of what needs to happen to save Composition—heightened methodological consciousness, methodological egalitarianism, and the re-establishment of Practice as inquiry (370–371)—is coming true, I suggest, and ironically the widespread adoption of an egalitarian ethnographic outlook has made it all possible.

Notes

1. English typography fails me here—I intend simultaneous reference here to both the generic making of knowledge and Stephen North's *The Making of Knowledge in Composition*.

2. North consistently maintains a careful distinction between "composition," the abstract common noun, and "Composition," a proper noun used to refer to the academic field of study. He writes, for example, "Any date, chosen to mark the beginning of 'modern' Composition is bound to be arbitrary. One might, for example, consider 1873,

the year Harvard first added an English composition requirement . . . " (1987, 9). Later on the same page, he makes his distinction explicit: "In a sense, there could be no Composition—academic field, capital "C"—before, say, 1958) (9). And later: "We can therefore date the birth of modern Composition, capital C, to 1963, 15).

3. The issue of terminology is especially troublesome. North writes, "Any number of terms have been or might be used in addition to the one [i.e., Ethnography] I have chosen. Consider this list of the more familiar: naturalistic, holistic, descriptive, qualitative, phenomenological, hypothesis generating (as opposed to hypothesis testing), participant observation, micro-ethnographic. . . . It is hard to locate this community's methodological heart or center. . . . For historical and political reasons, it is so far a community better defined at its borders, by its *contrasts* with other methodological communities, than by reference to any internal coherence: to say what Ethnographic inquiry is not than to say what it is. While its members and proponents embrace a range of methodological principles which have in common their divergence from positivist-based, and especially Experimental, principles, they do not mutually accept all of one another's principles and procedures" (1987, 274–275). While I acknowledge that there may be subtle (and occasionally useful) differences among these terms and concepts, I use them loosely as synonymous.

4. North's use of capitalization for his other subcatergories (or communities) of Composition is consistent with that of "Composition" and "composition." For example, on the same page, he writes, "knowledge produced by Practitioner inquiry" yet "the authority of the practitioner" (1987, 15). And writing of Kantor, Kirby, and Goetz's "Anthropological Research Models," he calls it a sort of rallying cry aimed at mustering what it can from past investigations under the banner of 'ethnographic studies,' hoping both to promote a greater understanding of extant work and, perhaps more important, to foster more of it.

Despite such a visible launching, though—lead article status in what must be considered Composition's leading Researcher forum—Ethnographic studies can hardly be said to have taken Composition by storm" (1987, 272).

I have followed North's capitalization practices (e.g., "Practitioner," "Research," and "Ethnography") throughout.

2

Ethnographic Practice as a Means of Invention
Seeking a Rhetorical Paradigm for Ethnographic Writing

Robert Brooke

The illusion that ethnography is a matter of sorting strange and irregular facts into familiar and orderly categories . . . has long since been exploded. What it is instead, however, is less clear.
Clifford Geertz

The ethnographer's narrative dilemma glosses over the epistemological crisis that authorship raises for the social sciences, namely, whether the researcher or the research method is telling the story.
Linda Brodkey

We must come to grips with the recognition that most ethnographic data is "produced" and not "found."
Roger Simon and Donald Dippo

Introduction

The more researchers in composition write reports we call ethnography, the more we wonder how to define this kind of research. Despite Kirsch's sensible plea for methodological pluralism (1992), debate over ethnographic method flourishes. Some scholars—foremost among them Steven Athanases and Shirley Brice Heath (1995)—argue that ethnographic studies of composition can be grounded in the long-standing practices of cultural anthropology. Other scholars, led by the early summary of qualitative methods by Kantor, Kirby, and Goetz (1981) for English education, contrast the "normal" categories of experimental science (reliability, generalizability, validity) to ethnographic practice with its focus on specific sites, particular detail, and possibly unrepeatable events, and argue for a hypothesis-generating as opposed to hypothesis-testing purpose for ethnography. Other writers, ranging from the politically quiet Geertz (1988) to radical pedagogues such as Simon and Dippo (1986) or Marcus and Fischer (1986), critique ethnography's claims to even a partial objectivity, arguing instead that every ethnography is the act of a politically/historically situated subject making choices to represent culture in one way or another. These writers all say they practice the same kind of research, but their descriptions of their principles and methods are so disparate it almost seems they are not talking to each other. No wonder Stephen North (1987) can say about ethnography, in one of his pithy summaries of research communities, "To put it quite simply, it is hard to locate this community's methodological heart or center" (273).

Although these researchers take different positions on the status and practice of ethnography, the grounds or context for their debates seems frequently the same. Thinkers begin with so-called *normal* scientific method and then contrast ethnographic method to it. For some, the deviations of ethnographic practice on issues of reliability, variable control, and researcher interference are problems to be managed (Kantor, Kirby, and Goetz, 1981). For others, these same features of ethnographic practice are not problems but virtues, giving the lie to "normal" science's claims to be free from such interference (Cintron, 1993). The grounds of the debate circle around the issue of *which kind of science ethnography is* (hybrid, nonscience, or definitional of what science really is). This issue becomes problematic because of *the rhetorical awareness of ethnographic researchers*, because they understand as writers the subjective, rhetorical nature of the act of writing in the production of ethnographic work.

These debates on the status of ethnography seem to raise two enduring issues for the field. First, they raise *the issue of representation and the question of power*—the issue of who represents whom, and to what effect in the social world? If, as Simon and Dippo argue, ethnographic data is "produced and not found," then consequent issues are the *adequacy* of the produced representation to the experience of those represented and the *sociopolitical function* of the produced representation. Ethnographic reports have consequences for people's lives: for the "natives" described, for the researchers doing the describing, and for the social institutions surrounding both. This issue and its question of power lurk behind the enduring problem of which kind of science ethnography is.

Alongside the issue of representation is a second issue: *the issue of writing and the question of invention*—the issue of how I, as a writer of ethnographic reports, "see" what I see, and the question of who I am as I write. If we ethnographers are not simply following an objective method as we write field notes and arguments to construct their "data," then what are we doing when we write? Where do the categories that prompt our inquiry come from; how do they change in the practice of our writing? Consequent issues are the very *possibility* of our seeing something as meaningful and the *location* of the writing self. This issue and its question of invention arise from the enduring problem of the act of writing in the production of ethnography.

It seems to me that the first issue, comprising representation and power, has been adequately explored. As several writers have explained, the issue of representation leads to a recognition of the impossibility of "objective" ethnography. Unlike so-called "normal" science, ethnography can never be free from the subjective, produced character of its representation. Given this impossibility, researchers who want to maintain the relationship between ethnography and science need to manage the interpersonal power relations that arise between representer and represented. Theorists offer at least three ways to manage these relations. Anthanases and Heath (1995) argue that the power relations surrounding representation can be managed by a careful return to anthropology's methods, functionally overcoming the issues of representation and power by making ethnography more like normal science. This answer seems to want to do away with the representation/power issue by retreating into a "better" scientific method. By contrast, most ethnographic theorists seek to embrace rather than escape the problematics of representation and power. Le Compte (1995), for example, argues that only in collaborative investigation, in which the persons being represented have a guiding say in the topics to be studied and the uses of the research, can these issues be ethically overcome. Because science can never be free from power relations, science must be made to serve those whom its gaze seeks to effect. In an extension of this line of thinking, Fine (1994) and McLaren (1992) each argue that the ethnographer can only resolve the issues of power and representation by the recognition that all research is at heart political, and therefore that ethical research requires a program of social transformation for greater freedom, dignity, and equality among peoples. Because science cannot be neutral, the politics of the researcher must be explicit. These three positions seem to me to offer the available responses to the issue of representation and the question of power. For ethnographers who seek to locate their work in relation to normal science, one of these three positions would be the stance they must take.

Unlike the relation of ethnographic practice to science, the question of the writer's work and location has only been partly described. Investigating this second issue, that of writing and the question of invention, is the purpose of this essay. To my mind, this second issue is less one of the relation of ethnographic practice to normal science and more one of ethnography's relation to rhetoric. Rather than looking to the adequacy of the representation in terms of the desired objective reality of the represented (as we do in probing ethnography's relation to science), the question of writing and invention asks us to examine the heuristic nature of ethnographic data, the Burkean terministic screens in which those data arise, and the developing rhetorical purpose for these data in the mind of the writer.

In this essay, I would like to begin an exploration of these more rhetorical issues in ethnography through an analysis of my own early participant-observation practice, in my work leading to the writing of my essay, "Underlife and Writing Instruction" (1987). I hope to show the deeply rhetorical nature of such work. In using my own practice as ethnographer as a site for analysis, I am following a long-standing tradition in anthropology, dating back at least to Malinowski's *A Diary in the Strict Sense of the Term* (1967) but certainly including contemporary writing such as Vincent Crapanzano's *Tuhami* (1980) and Majorie Shostak's *Nisa* (1981). In all this writing, ethnographers' attention to the production of their own work is used as a vehicle to probe questions facing the field.

If, as I believe, Bruno Latour (1987) is right in suggesting that *inscription* is one of the defining moments in all research because it is through inscription that what the researcher is studying becomes visible as a reified object in scientific prose, then it makes sense to think carefully about the moments of inscription in our own classroom studies. In the laboratories Latour studied, he found moments of inscription proliferating throughout scientific practice: in the instruments created so that bit of brain tissue can become physical data by inscribing itself in gel columns and assay chambers; in the statistical instruments used to transform these physical inscriptions into statistically-significant patterns; in the citation patterns from prior research used to create a context for these statistical inscriptions; and in the signatures of the researchers which invoke the presence of laboratories, grants, and status lurking behind the data; and so on. In my participant-observation practice, I can identify three moments of inscription, three places where I as researcher-writer "produce" the material that later becomes an article. These three moments are the *observation notebook* in which primary data from classroom activity or one-on-one interviews are recorded, the *reflective writing* in which I attempt, outside of observation, to construct or reconstruct some significance in my primary data, and the *article draft* in which I try to fashion a text for given readers from the material I have developed.

I would like to look at each of these inscriptive moments, using as an exploratory site my mid-1980s work as participant-observer in a colleagues' first year writing classroom. For the semester of the study, I attended each class meeting (recording observations in a notebook); I interviewed the teacher weekly outside of class and six students who were selected to provide a range of responses three times during the semester; and I spent an hour or two after each class period writing to make sense of what I was observing.

Observation Notebooks: Heuristic Categories and Where They Come From

What stands out to me about my practice of inscriptive moments in participant observation is that they all involve motivated choice. They are not full records of what happened moment-by-moment in the classroom or interview, but are *selections* from what happened. It is the *selective nature* of these inscriptive moments which makes the practice of participant observation, for me, so clearly a means of rhetorical invention.

The first choice facing a participant-observation researcher is what to record. Of all possible features of classroom interaction, which ones find their way into the researcher's notebook? I suggest that the nature of this choice is a form of selective description. The researcher tries to describe what occurs, but at the same time chooses which features to record based on some motivated sense of what might later prove significant.

Here, for example, is part of the first day of class notes from my study of a first-year writing classroom, the study on which my article "Underlife and Writing Instruction" was based:

First day of class

Read roster—some no shows
Introduced me—lots of smiles—
          all of us look nervous
—hedging on book—"formidable and tough"
one side of the room—all women—back all men
one wall mixed
          —men in back talk to each other in muffled tones (jokes?)
Janet [Teacher] nursing reading/writing connections
          M—informal writing and talk
          W—talk about books, informal writing in response
          F—Y[ounger]B[ecker]P[ike], small groups on papers
"Let you go ahead and read syllabus." (Many do now) "Any questions?"
          No questions right away
          —"copies of papers?"
"Why use maps? When last time?"
          —mostly silence
          —two students give common examples
"Think about early maps of Nebraska"
          —jokes
Monologue on maps—lots of academic vocabulary
          Map making as journal
          —"ask you to make an after-the-fact map"
          — "place where I lived as a child"
                    —"make map of neighborhood"
some response skeptical, others start right in, others enthralled
(She's doing a talk along as we're doing this, a patented suggestive prewriting)

[Here I drew the part of a childhood area map Janet was asking students to draw]
Janet has sat down in circle with rest of us
Some wandering eyes already—most maps are boxes, labeled
Now she's moving on to events/relationships there
There are some beginning draftsmen. Room remarkably quiet. —some friends (? two girls) sharing maps already room is set up as 3/4 circle around walls, with desk/blackboard against the fourth wall. An amphitheater effect. Wide open space for teacher. Janet has "business woman" dress jacket, skirt, white shirt—professional
Now she's drawing a map—most students are still doing theirs—one watching—some glancing at each other's—beginning to whisper now Janet's back is turned.
[notes continue for another two handwritten pages]

These notes show the ongoing tension between description and selection in the crucial inscription site of participant-observation work: the daily notebook. (I have changed these notes here only by altering the teacher and students' names to agree with the pseudonyms assigned them in my later articles, thus preserving anonymity.) Obviously, there is a lot more going on in the classroom than makes it into these notes. At times, I summarize what must have been much longer speeches on Janet's part (she's doing a talk along as we *do this*); at other places I notice one feature (*Janet's clothes*) without describing or finding relevant similar features (*student clothing*). My *recording attention* moves between recording what Janet does (*read roster*), to recording a range of behavior among the students (*beginning to whisper now that Janet's back is turned*), to recording the physical features of the classroom itself (*set up as 3/ 4 circle*), to summarizing pedagogical intentions (*Janet nursing reading/ writing connections*), to questions about student relationships (*some friends [? two girls] sharing maps already*). Obviously too much is going on in the classroom for me to record it all. What is recorded is selected from this much wider stream of events, perhaps even more selective than descriptive.

How does the selection process work? Looking over these notes, it seems to me that what guides the selection of what is recorded is a set of categories I had in the back of my mind for what might prove interesting. Some of these categories were derived from reading I had done in anthropology (which encouraged me, for example, to record the physical layout of the room). Other categories emerged from the interview I had with Janet before the semester began, in which she talked about her worries about a "teacher center stage role" and her use of Young, Becker, and Pike's textbook. That interview provides a reason I recorded her "hedging on YBP" and several things that positioned her in the classroom. Yet another category was clearly something like "student response" or "student interaction," given the number of entries I made about the range of such behaviors. Before I even began recording "data," I was "seeing" the classroom according to categories which produced the data I wrote down.

Two points strike me as important about the presence of such categories at this inaugural moment of inscription in the observation notebook. The first is the relation of such categories to the ancient rhetorical notion of an invention heuristic; the second is the location of the categories I used within the field of composition.

First, my use of categories to guide the selection of data matches quite closely with what the so-called *classical rhetorical tradition* identifies as invention heuristics: systematic methods for thoroughly exploring a subject before writing. From Aristotle (1954) on, the idea of invention as a part of rhetoric has been to treat separately and systematically the methods by which a writer might explore a rhetorical situation to find "the available means of persuasion." For him, the way to invent is to rely on categories of thought and experience (*topoi*) to search systematically for where "what can be said" might lie. His famous dual triumvirates (logos, pathos, ethos means of persuasion; ceremonial, legal, political occasions) and his list of commonplaces belong to the system of categories he creates. In Roman times, Quintillian would add the whole "stasis" theory for discovering which disagreements were central to the rhetorical situation and which were peripheral. In the Enlightenment, Scottish rhetoricians separated invention from the rest of rhetoric, leaving invention to the new-found systems of the "scientific method" then sweeping European consciousness. Throughout, the essential feature of a rhetorical approach to invention would thus remain the same: guided, systematic inquiry as a separate moment in the development of speech or writing, during which one searches for what might be said using categories of exploration you hope will prove fruitful.

In 1970, Young, Becker and Pike would claim the ancient word *heuristic* for systems of guided inquiry. An heuristic procedure, they claim:

> provides a series of questions or operations that guides inquiry and increases the chances of discovering a workable solution. More specifically, it serves three functions: 1) It aids the investigator in retrieving relevant information that he has stored in his mind. . . . 2) It draws attention to important information that the investigator does not possess but can acquire by direct observation, reading, experimentation, and so on. 3) It prepares the investigator's mind for the intuition of an ordering principle, or hypothesis. (120)

As I look over my observation notebooks from the mid-1980s, I see something like these invention heuristics guiding my initial recording of data in my observation notebooks. In my focus on categories of teacher behavior, student response, gender, and room layout rather than other possible categories of "data," I was clearly constructing a motivated representation of the classroom, identifying "data" that would serve a heuristic purpose for my thinking later on.

The second feature of these early categories I find interesting is that they all come from somewhere. They are categories I found interesting not because of something unusual in that first class (in fact, that class looked a lot like a host of other first classes I had taken part in, as teacher or student), but because of my location as a young researcher in the growing field of composition and rhetoric.

Carl Herndl (1991) invites ethnographers to consider their practice "as a professional activity" located in the "material conditions of institutions" (323), to examine in short the way the questions and values of the ethnographer's institutional location shape the activity she engages in. Looking at the categories I was using to record classroom data, I see the presence of such professional institutions in my own work. In the mid-1980s, I was fresh from completing a degree at the University of Minnesota, where I had assumed a sociolinguistic approach to problems of language. I had read a lot of Erving Goffman, pragmatic language philosophy, and developmental psychology as they applied to writing in college. Furthermore, the problem of student resistance to theory and pedagogy had been a major source of conversation in teachers' offices throughout my years at Minnesota. Against this backdrop, it makes sense that I "saw" evidence of different and competing "registers of language" when I looked at these classes, because this was what I was trained to see.

Reflective Writing: Sharpening and Limiting "Data"

As I look over the second inscription site in my participant observation notebooks, the reflective writing I did daily after class, I see myself writing primarily to understand the search categories I am using, and to refine them so that what I record will be more focused and relevant. After the first day of class, for example, I wrote:

> Students seem shy but willing to trust. Janet definitely established in a position of authority. Janet's role seems, at this point, to be the provider of information/topics/direction, I expect this will soon change, but for the moment she controls the conversation, elicits the kind of acceptable responses (both conversational additions and writing—students are informed what kind of story to tell, what kind of writing to do) and the student response is being quiet and occasionally whispering amongst themselves.
>
> As if there are two registers operating in the classroom—a teacher-level register, where info and responses are added to further the conversation the teacher imagines and directs, and a student-level register, where students talk amongst themselves about subjects/responses they choose.
>
> Janet is allowing for some crossover—the groups today had some talk sparked by teacher-direction but really student guided, and students left talking to one another. I expect a kind of crossover community to develop as the class progresses, where students will find they can talk in class in a register that is both theirs and the teachers. At the moment they're waiting to see 1) if the approach will connect to their experience and 2) if they can trust it—especially since Janet is asking them directly to try to connect the course to their experience with the first assignment.
>
> I wish I'd caught some examples of what students whispered to each other—I'll come earlier and sit more in the middle next time.
>
> Their quiet non-response to her direction is making her bend some—the only response she got to the maps question was stories of trouble—bad boy

behavior. Two such stories, which was partly the boys showing their peers they're rough, normal men. An interesting crossover.

In this reflection, I see myself refining what it is I am trying to record from this classroom, writing to explain or articulate the nascent selection categories I am struggling to use as I participate in this class. I am clearly interested in how the teacher positions herself, and in how various "registers" of language interact. I am clearly intrigued by what I call her "crossover registers" where student agendas and teacher agendas match, and by something I do not name yet in this reflection, the behaviors of students for purposes other than the teacher's. As a consequence of this writing, I make choices to focus my attention by coming earlier to catch "some examples of what students whispered to each other."

When I look ahead in my daily participant-observer notebooks, I see how this ongoing reflection about which categories of behavior to look for leads to more and more examples of whispered student conversation and uses of classwork different from the teacher's agenda. And these observations, in turn, guide my reflections after class, helping me sharpen the categories I am using for observation.

Two months into this study, for example, I systematically collect exchanges that showed student agendas clashing with those of the teacher. I record, for example, students referring to their papers as "that damn thing," one student teasing another about a particularly teacher-pleasing answer in a silent aside while the teacher wrote on the board, and the time a student shut her book during class and instead began writing a letter to a friend. These examples continue to provide evidence for one of the categories I began to explore the first day: the asides students whisper to each other, momentarily interrupting the normal flow of classroom events. As my class observations create more and more instances of these asides, my reflective class writing begins to speculate about them. Somewhere in the third month of the study, I began calling these kinds of behavior "underlife," using Erving Goffman's term. With time, some of these exchanges will find their way into the center section of my article "Underlife and Writing Instruction," in which I classify four kinds of student underlife and present examples of each.

What interests me about my reflective moments, and the way this writing feeds back into observation during the time of the study, is the way this writing is both productive and limiting at the same time. Productive: After making the connection between Goffman's term *underlife* and what I was seeing in this class, I returned to his text *Asylums* (1961) to reread his categories for underlife. I was able to lift his categories and begin going through my notebooks to classify the various forms of underlife I was seeing, to use those categories to organize the behaviors I was writing down, to look explicitly to see if certain kinds of underlife were or were not there. I soon discovered, for example, that I already had instances of all of Goffman's categories of *contained* underlife, but only Janet as teacher had exhibited any of his categories of *disruptive* underlife. Such refinement allowed me to return to the classroom with new observations to make.

At the same time, however, such connections limited observation as well. In the first few weeks of my observation notebooks, I began making observations concerning the category of gender, making some partial lists in my reflective writing of what male and female students were doing. But by the eighth week of my study, such observations and reflections had all but disappeared. Because I was now busy looking for something else (underlife), I moved into the periphery of my attention this other way of organizing experience (gender), which may have proved equally, if not more, interesting to trace. Now, in 1996, after having read Rubin (1993) and Tobin (1996) on gender in writing classes, I find myself mourning what I left behind in my notebooks, the enduring lacunae on this topic that frankly no longer exist in the data I collected. If, as Kenneth Burke argues, a way of seeing is also a way of not seeing, then clearly the invention issue for this second inscriptive moment surrounds the production and limitations of sight in the choice of which categories are refined and which left behind.

Writing a Draft: Locating Oneself Between Field and Subject

In my study, the third inscription moment occurred well after the end of the semester study, in the year following the classroom observation semester. During this period, I worked from my notebooks to draft an article for *College Composition and Communication*. The thesis sentence of that article, "Underlife and Writing Instruction," was:

> In contemporary writing instruction, both students and teachers undercut the traditional roles of the American educational system in order to substitute more complex identities in their place. . . . These forms of underlife, moreover, are connected to the nature of writing itself. (141)

This thesis sentence, however, was not what I first wrote. It emerged in a process of writing, every bit as rhetorical and complicated as the kinds of text-production Linda Flower (1994) has studied. As a beginning researcher yet to make my way in the field, I was drafting as much to create for myself a sense of readership, a sense of who the field might be, as I was working out the specifics of the underlife idea I had come to study.

Looking over the file of drafts that led to the underlife article, I am intrigued to find that Richard Gebhardt, then editor of *College Composition and Communication*, had me substantially revise the piece three times. All three revisions were aimed at locating the argument of the piece more adequately in relation to readers in the field of composition. In response to my first draft, Gebhardt wrote asking me to clarify the nature of the teacher-and-student roles I was writing about, considering "other approaches that alter the traditional teacher-student relationship: conference teaching, self-rating of papers, writing across the curriculum, computer assisted instruction." In response to my second draft, Gebhardt asked me to condense my summary of Goffman's work and to clarify the degree to which I was focusing on teacher or student underlife, or on both. In response to my third draft, Gebhardt asked me to revise one last time with an eye toward length, hoping I would find ways to trim the article down a little.

In the process of this ongoing negotiation with the editor and the outside reviewers he used, the article changed from a sprawling, forty-page draft (which included at least ten pages summarizing Goffman's work, in addition to copious examples from my notebooks) to a ten-page article that summarizes Goffman in two pages, student examples in four, and uses a series of boldface headings to guide the reader through the argument's structure.

What strikes me as interesting about this final inscription moment, the drafting process, is the degree to which it is characterized by negotiation of two kinds: on the one hand, a clear explicit negotiation between me as writer and the journal editor as reader, in which we had to negotiate the distance between our different knowledge and expectations; on the other hand, a less explicit internal negotiation I had to go through, attempting to make sense of my data in relation to three things: the argument I was developing, the classroom as I remembered it, and the *pressure* I was receiving from the journal editor as audience. In developing and revising this article, I had not only to negotiate a relationship with my readers, but also had to negotiate the emerging meaning of the text in relation to all the forces that impacted on it.

Brenda Jo Brueggeman has written eloquently about the writer's crisis such negotiation can bring about. Writing of her experience trying to complete a dissertation on an ethnographic study of Gallaudet, she explains:

> For a long time I tried, in vain, to write for two various audiences—my dissertation committee and the Gallaudet community. On the one hand, there was the academic (dissertation) audience. If I didn't address and represent them, I wouldn't be able to complete my dissertation, to earn the Ph.D. that had been my lifetime personal goal. Yet on the other hand, there was the "home" audience—the Gallaudet community and Deaf culture to which I now, in part belonged. If I didn't address and represent them, I wouldn't be likely to maintain my newly gained (and desired) identity among them. (MS 15)

Brueggeman poses the negotiation problem as a tension that arises because of membership in two communities and the difficulties of addressing/representing both. If, as she suggests, both audiences have their own discourse, their own way of articulating experience, then the ethnographer as writer is in an awkward position, needing to choose between them or forge a new discourse, potentially unreadable by either community.

It seems to me, however, that the rhetorical issue of negotiation, at the inscriptive moment of drafting, is even wider than Brueggeman describes here. It is not just an issue of negotiating between community expectations, but of negotiating a space within all the category choices already made, the mountains of recorded observations (all of which hide unrecorded other observations that could have been made), and one's own motivated interests as researcher. The inscriptive moment of such a draft seems to me to be about the very alteration of the writing self, in the sense that Michel Foucault (1979) describes in an essay on Descartes:

> Any discourse, whatever it be, is constituted by a set of utterances which are produced each in its place and time, as so many discursive events. . . . a meditation produces, as so many discursive events, new utterances which carry with them a modification of the enunciating subject. (19)

The patterns of data, argument, and audience expectations we uncover as we start drafting from our participant-observation research are complicated. They create a huge web of "discursive events" all of which carry with them "modifications of the enunciating subject." Like Foucault's meditator, the ethnographic writer finds herself entering such a web of modifying subjects when she immerses herself in her work that finds herself aware that she will not be the same kind of subject when she leaves the text as she is when she enters it. Thus, Brueggeman finds herself facing "for a long time silence" because whatever she writes will change how she herself and others perceive her. Thus, in working on the successive drafts of my article, I had to wrestle with the changes in myself (and my text) implied by the work I did. Who would I become, as teacher and writer, if I followed through the implications of this underlife stuff? Who would I become, as teacher and writer and member of the classroom community I had been in, if I explained what I had seen one way rather than another?

Conclusion: Rhetoric as Possibility

What I hope to have shown in the preceding pages is the deeply rhetorical nature of the inscriptive moments of my ethnographic practice. In my observation notebooks, the constructed nature of heuristic categories dominates; in reflective writing, the productive and limiting force of rhetorical focus; in drafting, the necessary and modifying existence of negotiation in relation to discourse and audience. All three inscriptive moments, in short, are rhetorical through and through.

As I said at the outset, my approach here seeks not to supplant an approach to ethnography through the question of what kind of science it is and how consequently to manage the troubling inadequacy of its representation. Instead, I have been seeking to explore a second issue related to ethnographic experience: the issue of writing and the question of invention. "Today," writes Brueggeman, "rhetoric, politics, and the personal are very much with us; and they are with us as we do fieldwork, as we write it down, write it up, and as we represent our selves and the "others" we study in this writing" (3). I agree.

For the writer embarking on a participant–observation project, rhetoric, politics, and the personal must necessarily be "with us," because the rhetorical nature of this work will lead us to rely on and question the categories we use to think, the choices we make about which categories to follow, and the selves we become as we try to explain to others what we've learned.

But therein lies the potential of ethnography, not as a tool or representational research, but as a tool of active rhetoric, functioning in the possible transformation of society. As Marcus and Fischer claim,

> It is here that the power of ethnography as cultural critique resides: since there are always multiple sides and multiple expressions of possibilities active in any situation, some accommodating, others resistant to dominant cultural trends or interpretations, ethnography as cultural criticism locates alternatives by unearthing these multiple possibilities as they exist in reality. (116)

Alongside the "crisis of representation" in ethnography, there is a corresponding opening for rhetorical action. The issues of representation and the writer, power and invention, supplement each other.

3

Ethnography or Psychography?
The Evolution and Ethics of a New Genre in Composition

Keith Rhodes

Preface: On Worrying About Words

This chapter argues provisionally for a new term to describe composition *ethnography*, offering the term *psychography*[1] to describe the nominally ethnographic practices of many composition researchers. By distinguishing these terms, I hope to expand our apprehension of the underlying practices being defined, both ethnography itself and the related, though more limited, *psychography*. Introducing a richer terminology for what composition's ersatz ethnographers really do should also help to contrast the underlying practices.[2] In particular, examining the emerging genre of *psychography* suggests renewed attention to the specific ethics of its practices. The potential for unconscious subjugation of the studied becomes more stark in psychography than is currently likely in ethnography—a function not only of the relative immaturity of psychography, but also of the narrower context within which psychography is practiced.

Of course, the terminology should not interest us so much as what we do. I do not care whether anyone actually adopts my proposed term, but its consideration should enhance the development and refinement of a valuable genre that bears only a distant familial relation to ethnography.

The Ethical Evolution of Ethnography
in Its Native Habitat

Compared with more traditional research methods, ethnography rightfully impresses composition scholars with its freshness, vitality, and wisdom. Still,

24

the field of ethnography has had its growing pains, too. As in literary criticism's movement from new criticism to post structuralism, ethnographers have run through a gamut of methods on their way to a practice that avoids both premeditated designs and pretensions of unbiased objectivity.

The results of ethnography's growth are impressive. Clifford Geertz (1984), perhaps as central to current ethnography as Aristotle was to classical rhetoric, defines a viewpoint that retains an ethical perspective while dispensing with the need to define ethnographic practice with formal purity. In his witty and profound formulation, "postmodern" disciplines like ethnography are founded not on any positive belief of their own, but on *anti-antirelativism*. Geertz first defines as *antirelativists* those who deplore the ways in which careful cultural study tends to undermine foundationalist assumptions. Resisting the charge of sheer relativism leveled by antirelativists, Geertz urges that the critical task of postmodern disciplines like ethnographic anthropology is instead anti-antirelativism, thus opposing antirelativist moral panic. Extrapolating from Geertz's argument, the instability of ethnographic theory is not rendered nihilistic merely because ethnographers do not define their practice once and for all. Turning the instability of their definitions to an advantage, ethnographic anthropologists generate an ethos that is de-centered and mediational but decidedly not a form of amoral "relativism." Indeed, ethnographers have made the ethical advantages of their mediational stance a point of departure—not only from other social sciences, but from the earlier anthropological investigation out of which ethnography has arisen. The relative maturity of ethnography as an anti-antirelativist discipline, then, offers hope that ethnographers can negotiate the instability of their work more reliably and more ethically at the same time.

Ethnography has thus moved through a struggle over disciplinary definition into a concern for ethical *praxis*. As George Spindler (1982) explains:

> Our discipline emerged as a by-product of a colonialized world where exotic "have-nots" were studied by scholars from the "haves." That we fostered receptivity for cultural differences and argued for cultural self-determination, encouraged respect for the integrity of other cultures, and worked against ethnocide is not to be denied. . . . But the fact remains that we collected knowledge, facts, and insights from the politically powerless peoples largely outside the benefit structure of modern economic and political systems. In doing so, we gained a better understanding of the world and built a discipline. Now it is time to apply the tools and insights of this discipline to problems that plague people everywhere, particularly people in our own complex, conflict-ridden, multicultural, dynamic society. We must study the poor *and* the rich, the mainstreamers as well as the minorities, and their interaction. (We have done better on the poor and the minorities than on the rich and the mainstreamers, so far.) (4–5)

In sum, ethnography has become implicitly ethical. At the very least, an overt attention to the ethics of ethnography is a prominent feature of ethnographic scholarship (Geertz, 1988; Van Maanen, 1988). Ethnography arguably has become the vanguard mediational and ethical discipline, the discipline most comfortable with the transactional nature of its knowledge and the pervasiveness of ethics in its *praxis*. Questioning why one does ethnography rather than how perfectly one is doing it becomes the pragmatic anchor that prevents ethnographic mediation from becoming mere relativism, generating the attractive maturity of ethnographic method.

Ethnography's Exotic Evolution in the Habitat of Composition

Understandably, ethnography's maturity attracts educational researchers, including researchers in composition and rhetoric. As Spindler (1982) puts it, "In fact, 'ethnography' has become a household word in professional education, and it is the rare research project today that does not have somewhere in the table of operations at least one ethnographer and somewhere in the research design some ethnographic features" (1). In educational research in composition, ethnography's effects have been pronounced, if diffuse. When it came to categorizing composition researchers, Stephen North included "ethnographers" as one of only four categories (1987, 272–313), despite finding few publications under that heading. And while composition researchers are cautious about claiming to do "ethnography," its methods have been diverted into composition's mainstream.[3]

Is there as much "ethnography" in composition research as it seems, though? Despite ethnography's central definition as a "hypothesis-generating" practice (Merriam, 1988, 3), in practice "ethnographic" research in composition often looks like hypothesis *testing*. That is, composition's "ethnographers" often bring specific theories to bear on limited observations. Moreover, these theories tend to be grounded in the literature known to the researchers, not in the culture of the observed—as illustrated in Geoffrey Cross's (1990) skillful use of a Bakhtinian framework to illuminate the patterns of corporate collaborative writing.[4] Although ethnography can contain some methodological messiness, to analyze a culture using previously studied theories rather than theories generated by the observation itself is a difficult stretch. This methodological stretch remains even when the previously studied theory fits the observations so well that the observations themselves suggest the theory, as in Cross's study.

In part, the stretching of ethnographic methods in composition is a function of the position of most tenure-track composition scholars. Despite being more like social scientists in theoretical matters, composition scholars must publish mainly in the personalized, heroic modes of humanists. Limitations in time, resources, and publication venues create circumstances in which composition "ethnography" often involves the researchers working part-time, observing one teacher and a few students a few hours a week for a few weeks.[5] Such an investigation has no chance to analyze a "culture" in ways that will "concentrate on the study of patterns—repetitive patterns of behavior and patterns of cultural knowledge" (Spindler 1982, vii). Hence, observers mainly see patterns already suggested by their own theories. Further, to call the observation of such patterns a study of "culture" is to overstate the extent to which students are a "culture" of class-takers. Quite the reverse, as Robert Brooke (1987) has demonstrated, a prominent feature of class "culture" is students' "underlife" behaviors and stances. Student underlife, drawn from the portions of their lives that have little to do with their studies, represents the actual culture with which students identify. Students understandably use "underlife" behavior to establish identities that resist the narrower "culture" offered by composition classes and theories.

Although "culture" plays a role in classrooms, then, the entire transaction is artificial, constructed by the very institutions that authorize the "ethnographic" studies. As a consequence, composition researchers attempt ethnography in circumstances in which its methods are difficult to apply. Unsurprisingly, they often check their findings against current theories to come up with a publishable "hook" for what they have learned. As a result, much "ethnographic" research simply tests existing theories. The resulting paradigm resembles that of traditional social science: placing subjects in an artificial, decontextualized environment, then observing whether they behave as preexisting theories would predict. "Ethnography" can thus become traditional social science, in which studies do not generate hypotheses but merely test them.

This mutated "ethnography" has even been validated as a normal research practice, a "qualified" form of hypothesis testing. Indeed, popular textbooks call such practices "qualitative research," distancing the practice even in name from the uncertainties of ethnography. One such text claims: "This book has been written to allow educators to design and carry out a problem-centered, situation-specific, qualitative case study" (Merriam, 1988, xiii), and later extols education as a field for qualitative research because it is "a familiar arena" (1). In other words, the culture no longer serves as the focus of learning at all. The "problem," a predetermined issue, becomes the focus, and the culture is seen as "familiar," fully understood in ways that supposedly can replace the need for a genuinely thorough ethnography. Even when such texts do claim the term *ethnography* and wrestle usefully with its implications, they are prone to undermine their good intentions. James Spradley's *Participant Observation*, otherwise lucid and astute, provides an archetypal example: a visual illustration contrasting "linear" traditional research with "circular" ethnographic research—with tidy, linear arrows drawn around the ethnographic circle (1991, 25–27).

Unsurprisingly, then, "ethnographers" within educational institutions often forget to generate new hypotheses based on their observations. Composition researchers may confirm, for instance, that the comma splice is a common usage "error," missing the underlying rhetoric of "comma splicing" that drives the usage. Preexisting assumptions can turn inquiry from understanding the cultural implications toward eliminating the usage. In effect, holding to preexisting hypotheses obscures the ethical concern that distinguishes ethnography from earlier forms of anthropology. The inquiry becomes less a question of "What is the cultural situation of writing education?" and more a question of "What is lacking in these students?" No matter how benevolently this last question is framed, it reeks of early anthropology that looked at the "deficiencies" of foreign cultures paternally.

The ethical dimension of ethnographic method is not merely an ethical issue because ethics are not merely ethical within the practice of ethnography. Researchers should not view hypothesis testing and hypothesis generating as neutral options for generating the same knowledge. Even so, the circumstances of educational research often force researchers to distill ethnography into simpler, hypothesis-testing "qualitative research."

Ethnography in Composition: A Dream Deferred?

To exemplify the state of composition ethnography, let us turn to a well-received work: "Peer Response in the Multicultural Classroom: Dissensus—A Dream (Deferred)," (1994) by Carrie Shively Leverenz.[6] Leverenz studied a classroom in which the teacher attempted to apply the theory of "dissensus" (as developed by Greg Myers and John Trimbur).[7] The article explains how dominant educational ideologies replicate themselves in unexpected ways, even within classrooms informed by alternative theories. Studying one small group intensively, Leverenz demonstrates how one student, an advocate of traditional approaches, suppresses the differences that might generate "dissensus" and cultural critique within her group. The group ends up reaffirming traditional notions of textual correctness and monolithic interpretation.

Valuable on its own merits, this article also presents with great clarity the methodological dilemma facing composition ethnography. Leverenz uses unusually astute ethnographic sensitivity in her approach to gathering and interpreting her information. At a critical point, though, she turns her discussion toward refinements in applying the theory of "dissensus," dreams of which are "deferred" by its clear failure. In other words, a pre-determined theory is made the privileged subject of the discourse, with the students eventually coming to serve as something disturbingly like subjects of traditional, hypothesis-testing research. Leverenz herself does not generate the "experimental" conditions, of course. She is, however, an authorized agent of larger institutions; at that larger, institutional level the experimental paradigm appears in very pure, if reduced, form: a situation is constructed according to a theory, and the effects of that theory are then examined.

It would be absurd to say that Leverenz, who controls only the obser-vational and representational parts of the "experiment," has any ethical culpability. Leverenz uses, responsibly and well, an approach established by other prominent composition ethnographers: applying authoritative theory terms of famed theorists to extensive classroom observation. Further, Leverenz teaches vital lessons. The reprinting of her article in a book representing the best of ten years' scholarship in *Journal of Advanced Composition* confirms the exceptional quality of her research. The success of Leverenz's work within its paradigm indicates very clearly that her disjunctive claim of having a preconceived theoretical agenda and an ethnographic approach is the mark of utterly normal, even exceptional, composition research.

What Leverenz has done, however, escapes definition as ethnography, despite being defined as "an ethnographic study of peer response" (256). Indeed, Leverenz indicates her own methodological ambivalence, elsewhere terming her method "microanalysis" and admitting that the portion of classroom culture her study has investigated is "too small to invite generalizations" (256). That being the case, no hypotheses could be generated by the research; instead, as was done, hypotheses could only be brought to the research to be tested. As a result, it is not surprising that the students in Leverenz's study are represented largely as unreflective social objects who are constructed by institutional and theoretical forces. Interestingly, though, the more fully realized identity Leverenz assumes for herself, perhaps with some misgivings, implicitly argues that she transcends these same institutional and theoretical currents. In other words, Leverenz seems to upset normal ethnographic conventions most essentially by writing from a position of assumed cultural superiority—a position the reader is invited to share. This invitation, in turn, is hard to decline because it is implicit in composition education. It is one that we readily accept in planning courses for "our" students—evoking allegorical images of preethnographic anthropologist E. E. Evans-Pritchard leading "his" Azande into battle on behalf of England (Geertz, 1988, 49–72). The use of privileged theories simply extends this paradigm of privilege in ways composition teachers accept and hope to use. Indeed, I have found this article to be extraordinarily useful, one of a small handful to which I regularly refer while planning new ways to approach my writing classes. To the extent that there is a departure from the defining ethical core of ethnography in Leverenz's article, then, it is a departure in which complicity is widely shared.

This complicity renders most disturbing the inevitable negative aspects of the genre Leverenz uses, whatever we call it. Perhaps the most telling moment is the final analysis of "Beth," the pseudonymous antagonist who most strongly opposes the dreams of "dissensus." Beth continually works against the wider explorations of literacy encouraged by the class, forcing her small group to attend to traditional, narrow issues of "correctness" and standard interpretation. Leverenz explains Beth's actions in this way:

> . . . Beth's voice, after all, is the voice of the institution. It is the voice of every teacher who had ever given her an "A" for abiding by the established conventions and norms of academic writing. More to the point, perhaps, Beth's voice is our voice. Hearing Beth speak in that voice proved especially unsettling to me, for she was a flesh-and-blood embodiment of institutional power, one who acted consistently to maintain the status quo and to silence difference. Even more troubling is that Beth, a bright and thoughtful student,

had been taught to maintain the status quo without what many teachers see as an equally crucial lesson: the capacity for self-reflection that would have enabled her to see the consequences of her behavior for herself, her peers, and ultimately her society. (Leverenz, 1994, 271–272)

In lamenting this "unsettling" phenomenon, though, Leverenz ignores signs of the same phenomenon elsewhere in the transaction. The teacher, too, is the instrument of theorists whose institutional power has led the teacher to replicate a theory. We cannot know how reflectively the teacher may have adopted these theories. Still, the teacher's position and Beth's are comparable; after all, both Beth and the teacher seem likely to report their own actions as "willing."

The issue of will, in fact, becomes even more problematic when we view the larger transaction among teacher, students, and researcher. Even Leverenz may be in a position of questionable agency. She is paradoxically unwilling to ask outright whether the theory of "dissensus" itself has been disproven.[8] Leverenz, from her authorized position, concludes that unreflective "status quo" motives are working through Beth. Yet perhaps Beth understood her situation quite well, using a traditional role as an oppositional underlife. Far from being a rubber stamp for traditional theories, Beth could be signaling her genuine autonomy, her independence from the student role prescribed for her in the dissensus-driven classroom. Beth, after all, boldly asserts her "status quo" position while Leverenz, the authorized observer, looks on. Indeed, to get too carried away for a moment, one could imagine this article as part of the underlife of a graduate student researcher posing a quiet but stark challenge to a powerful contingent within the field that has constructed her own position. Yet this potential critique of "dissensus" itself is muffled. Under the logic of this imaginary thread, Beth could be the most overtly self-conscious, free-willed player in the fully dramatized scene of the article.

Thus, a full ethnographic study of these interactions would need to expand in several directions. The researcher would need to examine Beth's background and her behavior in other classrooms. The researcher would have to explore the institutional settings in which the class was planned and the study itself was authorized. The researcher would need to look into composition's disciplinary apparatus, in which decisions are made about what kind of articles get written and published. These last, of course, represent the realms of power where fully ethical ethnographers need to tread. In composition "ethnography," we rarely see this expanded scene; ultimately the result affects the agency and will of the readers themselves. The result of an article's being less than a genuine ethnography appears not to be merely that it does not fit some arbitrary definition. Rather, the practical effects the study could have are profoundly affected, and possibly in ways that restrain the direct criticism of composition theories. What Leverenz has found so unsettling in Beth's voice is, as a result, eerily echoed in the processes generating the article itself.

Ethnography, Psychography, and the Ethics of Composition Research

Examining even an exemplary composition "ethnography" reveals that what composition "ethnographers" do, even at best, does not preserve much meaning for the term. "Ethnography" in composition does not explore cultures so much as it explores individual experience within closely defined cultural institutions. Perhaps most critically, such research does not seem to preserve the same mediational and ethical *praxis* that has generated the attractive freshness and value of ethnography. These departures have significant consequences. In ethnography, combining thickness of description with critical self-awareness encourages a fully participatory critical reading. Consequently, both the subjects of the study and the readers share in the resulting construction. Ethnography, then, is neither "objective" nor "subjective," generating a profound "anti-antirelativist" shared "author-ity." While ethnography is founded on a distrust of objectivity, then, its mediational *praxis* has rigors of its own. A method that seeks to undermine even unknown biases should have no room for the enforcement of intentional ones. Thus, the ethical goal of avoiding cultural hegemony in ethnography is not simply moral; it strengthens the methodology itself. By contrast, "ethnographic" studies in composition consistently focus on predetermined goals and make persistent reference to theories developed outside the culture under study. Hence, such studies profoundly alter the methodology they claim to use.

Even so, the answer is not asking composition scholars to be more perfectly ethnographic. Clearly, the high-water mark of ethnographic method in English studies has been Shirley Brice Heath's *Ways With Words* (1983). Heath, of course, is a fully experienced ethnographer who had time for extensive investigation. Her study of two different language communities in their home environments would be completely beyond the reach of nearly all practicing writing teachers. Further, not only is Heath's method beyond practical reach, her results, though impressive, do not mean that only full-blown ethnography has value. Heath's study sometimes strains to say anything practical about literacy education beyond what should already be common knowledge—that punishing students for using "home" language is often unjustifiably brutal. Indeed, the main practical suggestion Heath ends up making is simply that ethnographic practice may itself be an ethical and effective composition pedagogy. In what sense her work augments other, more reduced exhortations for collaborative pedagogy and community literacy is difficult to tell. Important as Heath's work is in a larger sense, then, it has powerful negative implications for the future of fully ethnographic composition research. Balancing the difficulties of "ethnographic correctness" with its gains seems to counsel against setting such a rigorous methodological standard as a necessary goal within composition research.

Hence arises the proposal that those who read and write composition "ethnography" could benefit from renaming their new genre. Clearly, there is a new genre, a new relationship among purposes, audiences, and subjects. That this new genre merits a new term should not trouble sophisticated postmodern sensibilities. There are seeds of absurdity in ignoring the failure of composition "ethnographers" to use ethnographic methods, have ethnographic purposes, or share ethnographers' central ethos. Composition "ethnography" simply is not thickly described writing that explores whole cultures, or even whole subcultures. Instead, Leverenz and others have already begun to establish "psychography" as a distinct genre: thickly described writing exploring the connections of individual psyches with specific cultural conditions. Janet Emig (1971) and Mina Shaughnessy (1977) perhaps began this trend, bending traditional forms of educational scholarship and social science to bring the complexity of student experience into the formation of theories. Acclaimed psychographies-before-the-name by such writers such as Stephen North (1986),[9] Robert Brooke (1987), and Joy Ritchie (1989, 1990) built on this break and generated a new form. This new form has developed its own conventions: reasonably extended study, moderate thickness of description, small focus groups, collaborative separation of teacher and researcher roles, self-conscious personalizing of all participants, and genuine concern for the dignity of the students and teachers being observed. The best psychographers use these conventions to generate a "double-voiced" text in Bakhtin's sense (1981, 324–325), a text in which disparate voices create the possibility of readings that may (and at times even must) escape the intentionality of the author. It is in this heteroglossic effect that the best "psychography" still deserves a name that evokes ethnography.

From this perspective, Leverenz's study is a model of new ideals toward which researchers can strive in the developing genre of "psychography." Leverenz clearly does explore in useful detail one of the more critical issues in composition, and does so with a usefully rich cultural and personal perspective. Her concern for the best interests of students is deep and informed. The more telling criticisms of the article, in fact, involve primarily the state of a new genre. Studying subjugated educational "objects" in service of authorized theories, a task the current form of the genre virtually demands, tends to work an inescapable and subtle violence against those being studied. This subjugation, built into educational institutions themselves,[10] overwhelms best intentions to the contrary. Nevertheless, Leverenz counters this built-in subjugation by using effective "psychographic" technique: bringing the individuals into cultural relief, revealing complicated individual positions in social dynamics, and framing her own social position in the narrative. Leverenz creates a "double-voiced" essay, one which bears repeated and dialogic reading. Had Beth been a statistic and Leverenz a statistician, the real issues would be invisible. Had Leverenz dramatized personal impressions, the rich patterns she explores would remain obscure. Had Leverenz held out for nothing short of full ethnography, most likely she would still be writing her book-length treatment. In short, psychography, done well, is valuable.

Even so, ethnography's spirit of ethical mediation probably needs greater emphasis in psychography. In ethnography, generating theories, perceptions, and explanations requires collaboration among subjects, writer, and readers. In psychography, there should be a similar willingness to value the ways of the studied and question the ways of the studying. Psychographers should always remember that applying explanations from elsewhere is automatically a move toward objectifying and colonizing the studied. Leverenz does work to retain the ethics of ethnography within her work. Still, it would be intriguing to see what results she might have produced had she allowed her own central observation—the operation of dominant theories through the unwilled agency of individuals—to be examined simultaneously in her own experiences and those of the teacher. For instance, the teacher's motivation to construct a "dissensus"-driven class might have presented a pattern of doubt that was provocatively different from Beth's unflagging allegiance to tradition, or it might have presented an equally provocative parallel.

Of course, had Leverenz de-centered her privileged theorists in this way she might also have rendered her article unpublishable. Thus, it does seem to matter that Leverenz and her publishers were not able to call her a psychographer (or something like it). As things stand, we as readers are tempted to normalize power constructs we ought to question. As an author, Leverenz implicitly assumes a degree of willed agency that Beth is denied. Indeed, it is not clear that Leverenz would feel entitled to "author-ity" without an assumed theoretical superiority; nor is it clear that her publishers would have accepted anything any less "author-itative."

Conclusion: Controlling the Development of Psychography

Positioning this exact ethical quandary of "author-ity" in the foreground is ultimately more important than adopting the term *psychography*. Still, without a terminology that indicates clearly just where limited composition "ethnographies" depart from their namesakes, it may prove difficult to deal better with the problem of the play of power and will in composition research. Thus, the naming game may actually be of some use here. Indeed, beyond naming and recognizing "psychography" as a new genre, perhaps there is no reason to control its development. Clearly, there is already a new genre that is neither fully ethnographic nor merely "qualitative research." It is a usefully messy genre in which postmodernism meets both the continuing need to hear "expressivist" individual stories and the "positivistic" need to validate hypotheses. Psychographers already mediate between antifoundationalist criticism and the need to make positive statements in order to carry on a practice of teaching. Perhaps "psychography" is just good scholarly practice in need of naming, a genre that already handles well the inconsistencies and paradoxes of "anti-antirelativism" as applied to composition teaching.

Such a genre probably needs more nurturing than policing. There remains a need for further experimentation, for risk taking, and for creative vision on the part of teacher researchers who take it up. Indeed, the most promising source of valuable psychography may be extensively experienced teachers who do not often keep up with theoretical scholarship. Consequently, there is a corresponding need for scholarly publishers in composition to take risks too, particularly by taking seriously psychographic articles that may not "round up the usual suspects," dutifully citing fashionable theorists. The shaping of a new genre rarely follows any clear precedent with tidy predictability. The extent to which a work is upsetting, unsettling, disturbing, even apparently "naive," might come to favor its publication, not work against it. Given the high quality of pioneering "psychography" thus far, we could probably benefit from less rather than more regulation of further work.

If there is an area requiring conscious regulation, it lies less in the area of "scholarly substance" and more in the ethics of using representational power. As ethnographers also discovered, ethical balance comes not from moralizing, but from facing that which unsettles belief. As Geertz writes (1984), "Looking into dragons, not domesticating or abominating them, nor drowning them in vats of theory, is what anthropology has been about" (275). Ethnography's methodology of unsettling the beliefs of the culture doing the studying imports a central ethical purpose into its practice, implicitly working against a smug colonialism. While Julius Caesar's accounts of his Helvetian campaign might meet strictly functional standards for cultural study, waging war against the subjects of one's study (or even waging war using them) would violate the spirit of ethnography. Similarly, composition research reminds us that language is inherently ideological, and that "neutral" attention to "correct" behavior (by either traditional or alternative standards) often masks ethical barbarism.

Composition's theoretical growth has some relationship to that of ethnography, then, finding part of its genesis in opposing an "antirelativist" tradition of linguistic colonization. Still, having theoretical designs on the subjects of study, as in most composition research, is at odds with ethnography. This should concern composition "psychographers" Caesar studied the Helvetians as a target for conquest, largely passing over the great vivacity of their cultural and spiritual life. As Robert Brooke (1991) points out, student underlife is not merely an obstacle to be overcome; it also represents an opportunity for cultural dialogue (81–82). Composition researchers' ideological, "imperial" blind spots are produced most often by our deep allegiance to theories. Research that remains rooted in our theories more than in the lives of students threatens to keep student underlife perpetually "under": under represented, under subjugation, and underfoot. Working in narrower contexts, psychographers may need a more specific ethical stance than ethnography's "anti-antirelativism."

There are no easy answers. The immediate remedy, however, may lie less in an ethic of protection than in one of humility. Too much "ethical correctness" could undermine this developing genre. We can tolerate more ethical callousness in psychography than in ethnography. Psychographers use representational power toward specific and limited ends and do not define one entire culture in the eyes of another. Beth, protected by her pseudonym, probably encounters little risk relative to the value of Leverenz's contribution to knowledge about peer groups, dissensus, and research in composition. The very circumstances of current educational institutions ensure a certain degree of oppression, something revealed by psychographic practice, not created by it. To demand ethical purity from psychographic research and publication would be essentially to kill the messenger. It would seem, though, both fair and valuable for researchers to write themselves into their studies in roles that are not presumptively privileged. If we must still be satisfied with doing rather better at representing the subjugated than representing the authorized, the least that composition's psychographers can do is to put themselves in both positions—subjugated and authorized—simultaneously. Such authors need to (and need to be permitted to) write in ways that invite and even initiate critique of their own work. I am not sure most of the more prominent publication venues are ready for such antiheroic discourse. Based on the quality of the work in this lineage, however, I suspect that the quality of the resulting work would richly reward those that are.

Notes

1. This term has been brought into composition studies in another context by Debra Journet (1993a; 1993b). Journet, though, does not define a genre likely to be used extensively in composition studies but rather defines a genre of medical writing.

2. If the issue were exploring the meaning of "ethnography" itself, perhaps a better approach would be the collective definition of "keywords" surrounding ethnographic practice. Prime examples of keyword approaches are Raymond Williams's (1976) treatment of terms surrounding "culture" and the work of Kathleen Welch (1990) (citing Williams as a strong inspiration) in classical rhetoric. Constructive work with a collection of keywords, however, would require bringing several terms into play in context with each other, a difficult task in treatments shorter than book-length. Perhaps more important, my main argument is not that language has shifted meanings and needs redefinition but that an important term has failed to develop.

3. Tabulating "ethnographic" articles is hampered by the very problems of definition that this article addresses. That is, some articles studying rather few subjects rather incompletely bravely embrace the term, while other, more thorough investigations give it scant mention. In a Boolean search of the ERIC database for 1982 through March of 1996, I found 298 articles that matched the search "ethnograph* and writing" and 198 (often duplicates from the first search) that matched the search "ethnograph* and composition." The clear majority concerned composition pedagogy. A significant

number, however, were more in the nature of this article—a theoretical discussion rather than an ethnographic investigation.

4. Cross (1994) himself presents an informed discussion of this very problem in a later article.

5. Even many of the most extensive and acclaimed investigations fit within the outer ranges of this definition (Brooke, 1987; Ritchie, 1989; Ritchie, 1990; Leverenz, 1994).

6. This article was originally published in *Journal of Advanced Composition*; I cite the later version published in Olson, Gary and Stanley I. Dobrin, 1994, *Composition Theory for the Postmodern Classroom* (Albany, NY: State University of New York Press), 254–273.

7. Leverenz refers to dissensus as "an approach to collaborative learning that attends to the nature of difference and dissent that exists within groups" (255). Essentially, Myers and Trimbur posit that collaborative work becomes more valuable as cultural critique when the common collaborative goal of consensus is replaced by one of "dissensus."

8. While Leverenz does note that "dissensus" has had little practical development (255), nowhere does she suggest that it may be a flawed idea.

9. North (1987), who defines "ethnography" very strictly, classifies his own article as "criticism," a transfigured form of literary hermeneutics (118). Still, there are many parallels between North's study of three philosophy students and the other articles discussed here. North explains his intention as wanting "to explain the writers and their writings in terms of one another, and in a way that accounted for the peculiar milieu in which they worked" (121).

10. As Leverenz herself notes, "Critiques of the normalizing function of institutionalized discourse communities must begin, therefore, by challenging the assumption that any setting within the academy represents one of 'non-domination' " (272).

4

Composition's Appropriation of Ethnographic Authority

Kristi Yager

"There is a curious time lag as concepts move across disciplinary boundaries. The moment the historical profession is discovering cultural anthropology in the (unrepresentative) person of Clifford Geertz is just the moment when Geertz is being questioned in anthropology."

—Paul Rabinow 1986

This quote aptly reflects my own conclusions about how ethnography has been appropriated by composition studies. In this case, composition, not history, has discovered cultural anthropology when, indeed, it should be discovering critical anthropology as well. Represented by such theorists as James Clifford, Clifford Geertz, Mary Louise Pratt, and Renato Resaldo, critical anthropologists examine the discursive elements of ethnographic methodology to discover the underlying assumptions of a given ethnographer's work. Using the term as circulated in the critical theory originating with the Frankfurt School of social thought, *critical anthropologists* seek to uncover the power-knowledge relationships that structure and determine a given author's meaning.

While the field of composition studies has embraced critical theory, phenomenological teacher-research theory and ethnography could benefit from examining their practices through the lens critical anthropologists offer. By presenting how the protagonists of critical anthropology—the crisis over authority and the crisis over representation—have been unknowingly imported into composition research, I hope to persuade composition's teacher researchers to embark on alternative authorial identities. My argument is

37

analogic, suggesting that anthropologists and composition's teacher researchers face the same problems, problems best explained and exemplified through two tropes that have been employed to establish authority and to represent others. These are the literary tropes of the hero which, in ethnographic writing typically take one of two forms: the "royal arrival" or the "old-fashioned castaway" (Pratt, 1986).

In our first anthologies of teacher-research, [*Reclaiming the Classroom* (1987), *Seeing for Ourselves* (1987), and *The Writing Teacher as Researcher* (1990)] *teacher-research* was defined as "systematic and intentional inquiry carried out by teachers" in order to professionalize teaching, invest practitioners with more authority and control in classrooms, schools, and ultimately the fields of education and English studies at large" (Cochran-Smith and Lytel, 1990).

A better definition of teacher-research exists, however, in James Berlin's introduction to *The Writing Teacher as Researcher* (1987). Berlin argues that "teacher research in the United States must emphasize and problematize its political agenda . . . it must see schools as places where ideological and political battles are enacted . . . and it must address this matter directly" (10).

Like Berlin, I think compositionists should look abroad to the theorization and practice of teacher-research in Britain and Australia where it is called "action research." In those countries, scholars define *teacher-research* as part of a radical pedagogic endeavor which seeks to change the power-knowledge structures of a society through radically democratizing learning. Part of this agenda is to view teacher-research as an ethnographically-oriented research which forwards a phenomenological epistemology and is rooted in a social constructivist tradition.[1]

The argument presented here rests on a phenomenological foundation, which, very briefly put, means that my argument advocates a narrative epistemology. It stresses that knowledge is situated and grows out of the personal perspective of the researcher. Grossly simplified, a narrative epistemology maintains that subjectivity cannot be divorced from objectivity, and the terms, operating almost exclusively as polarities, have little value for humanistic inquiry such as anthropology or composition studies. Instead, a phenomenological or narrative approach upholds *contextually* based research. It offers a value claim that emphasizes an understanding of what happens in a "specific place, at a particular time, and under certain circumstances" (Resaldo, 1989, 131).

Luckily, to discuss the division of expertise and objectivity on the one hand and experience and subjectivity on the other has become a commonplace among scholars who want to redress this Cartesian dualism by first proving its illogic and second by outlining those possibilities the rejection of such a dualism affords. In anthropology, Clifford, Geertz, Pratt, and Resaldo have found that despite ethnography's claim to a kind of phenomenological epistemology (ethnography is, after all, the study and representation of *human* experience), most ethnographies still forward a dualistic epistemology that splits subject from object and devalues the former to the latter. This leads them to ask how an ethnographer can even claim to represent the lived experience of others? Critical anthropologists attempt to explain this by centering critiques around the issues of authority and representation. For this purpose, Michel Foucault's "What is an Author?"[2] (1977) provides an adequate starting point.

According to Foucault, two meanings hide within the concept of "author." An author is both an authorizer, a person who gives credence to certain practices and ideas, and a writer, concerned with the way reality can be created and represented by textual strategies. Foucault argues that more often than not, the method of textual production rather than the writer is cast as the narrator of a text. The text, in other words, gains its authority by calling on an esteemed methodological history. Foucault primarily supports his claim by proving that since the nineteenth century, only Marx and Freud can be called authors because only they initiated discursive practices: other theorists have acquired authority for their statements from either Marxism or psychoanalysis.

Pratt's "Fieldwork in Common Places" (1986) explains how canonical enthnographic writers have (perhaps unconsciously) drawn on the rhetoric of certain "methodologies" in discourses adjacent to ethnography (e.g., travel writing, missionary writing, colonial official documents, and personal memoirs).[3] Her use of the term, *commonplace*, in the title can only be meant to pun on that word's etymology, for it clearly refers to the intellectual placeholders in anthropological history, who, in Foucault's sense, now authorize certain methodologies—Bronislaw Malinowski, the "father" of modern ethnography, and his pupil, Raymond Firth, and Sir Edward Evans-Pritchard and his student, David Maybury-Lewis. These are more than two pairs of individual names. Each set represents a way of doing and writing ethnography, one that draws on a historical context (the writing existent for a specific area) and a rhetoric. Pratt contends that ethnographers do not really portray a foreign culture as much as they reproduce the familiar rhetorical and narrative structures inherent to adjacent "home" discourses.

She illustrates her point by breaking down into two categories the primary elements of most ethnographies: *personal narrative* and *objective description.* She then shows how ethnographers use one (personal narrative) to create a justified space for the other (objective accounts). In this manner, anthropology has upheld a Cartesian dualism in its ethnography despite its desire to re-*present* the lived experiences (and presumably, therefore, the ideologies) of others. Pratt goes on to explain that the ethnographer usually begins his account of the field with a *tale of entry*, what Geertz calls the *being there* authority of a text. As a commonplace, the "tale of entry" takes the form of a royal arrival or the old-fashioned castaway story. Malinowski and Firth (who worked in the South Pacific) use the trope of a royal arrival to narrate an essentially ideal experience of acceptance and accommodation.

Evans-Prichard and Maybury-Lewis, however, worked in Africa, where the conditions and the native culture were more hostile than those experienced by Malinowski and Firth. In a more-than-coincidental corollary, both Evans-Prichard and Maybury-Lewis use the trope of the "old-fashioned" castaway to begin their ethnographies and to set up the premise for the "master-slave" relationship with the people "under" study, which predominates their narrative (36–39).

These tropes—especially the trope of the castaway—are often used in composition's teacher-research. As a means of introducing the radical pedagogy of *Empowering Education* (1992), Ira Shor opens the first chapter with an image of himself as a child, the innocent-in-the-know, the kid possessing the knowledge educators now need. Here, he describes how he loved learning but not schooling (he would look out the window to happily see the school disappear into a gray fog bank).

As an image for the first day of class, Shor's self-reflection introduces his sense of captivity in a hostile environment that he must somehow "tame" in order to educate the "natives":

> I entered B building on our concrete campus and climbed the stairs . . . . My writing class was in room 321, a place I knew well, with its gray tile floor, cinder-block walls, dirty venetian blinds, fiberglass chairs, and cold fluorescent lights. . . My confidence was shaken a little that first day when I reached the open door of B-321 and heard—not a sound. Was this the right classroom? Had my room been changed at the last minute? I took a step forward, peeked in the door way, and saw twenty-four students setting dead silent . . . All eyes turned in my direction. There were many eyes, but no smiles. New York, my home town, is famous for its tough faces, but these were some of the toughest I had ever seen on students. (2)

After introducing himself, Shor suggests students put their chairs in a circle to make talking easier, but no one moves.

To me, this seems like a kind of castaway tale—though exactly who is being cast away—the teacher (by the students) or the students (by the educational system) is not yet clear. In fact, perhaps this double entendre is the necessary opening for Shor, since it immediately deemphasizes his authority and puts him in a position to emphasize the commonalities between him and his "group" of students.

In fact, the title of the first chapter, "The First Day of Class: Passing the Test," can be interpreted as double entendre as well, for clearly, Shor wants to "pass the test" of acceptance so crucial to a radical pedagogue's sense of purpose, as well as to "pass the inherent test of interest" with which readers approach a text.

The chapter title also refers to those students who find themselves in Shor's remedial writing class because they have failed the university placement test.

In *Writing Relationships: What Really Happens in the Writing Classroom* (1993), Lad Tobin begins with a similar tale:

> I'm tired and ready to go home; of course, I thought I was tired and ready to go home this morning, after teaching two sections of Freshman Composition

and one of Literary Theory. But that was nine conferences ago. And that was before I read some awfully rough drafts on why the drinking age should be lower, why a dog really is a man's best friend, why affirmative action is just legalized discrimination . . . . (1)

Chapter Five marks the last section of Part I, "The Student Teacher Relationship," and tellingly, Tobin hasn't seemed to move from his initial attitudinal stance:

> It is 8:25 a.m. and I am sitting in a cold, dark classroom watching my students shuffle in. Outside is a sleeting rain and I briefly indulge myself in the fantasy that I am feeling the same "damp, drizzly November in my soul" that Ishmael describes in the opening of *Moby Dick*—although his feeling drove him to sea in search of the great white whale, while I, decidedly landlocked, sit at a small metal student desk in an antiseptic room that I suddenly realize has none of the things that make a place comfortable. By 8:22, I realize something else: eight of 24 students have apparently decided to cut class. The sixteen who have shown up look as miserable as I feel. (75)

In this abysmal tale of entry, Tobin identifies with the first-person narrator of a heroic tale; a hero who finds himself frustrated in his search for truth and meaning because, we later find out, of the weather, the fact that students did not do their homework, and that Tobin has taught the poem under study far too many times to muster much enthusiasm for it.

Both Shor and Tobin narrate experiences of imprisonment: in their descriptions of their surroundings, of the students, or of their work. And both, interestingly, cast themselves as frustrated heros, questing for a pure and true learning environment or experience, but unable, initially, to overcome their shock and disappointment. These examples of castaway tropes are by no means the exception to the rule. Think of Jane Tompkins' "Me and My Shadow," Mary Rose O'Reily's "Exterminate the Brutes," Cynthia Biery's "When All the Right Parts Don't Run," or Deborah Chappel's "The Stories We Tell."

This naturalistic research also uses the royal arrival trope, though it usually appears after the introduction and may not, in fact, appear until well into the book. Let me explain. Most teacher research combines personal narrative with a kind of "science of self help," (the how-to/objective-instruction part of the book) in such a way as to suggest a kind of royal arrival: just follow these quick and easy steps and you, too, can transform your classroom from a state of hostility to one of happy collaboration. In Shor's and Tobin's books, the narratives start out badly, but end happily. The books are tales of transformation—though who actually gets transformed is an issue I will explore momentarily.

Such introductory personal narratives as these make a pathetic appeal: they seek to arouse the reader's emotions and to establish the writer's ethos as credible. Because the ethnographer "went there" (and suffered), and because as teachers we commonly unite around such tales of woe, we find ourselves immediately receptive to such narrative accounts.

After such bold openings, however, the ethnographer usually disappears from the text, hidden behind objective pronouncements of the students or "culture" under study. The ethnographic body itself makes an appeal to logos: the ethnographer represents him or herself as an impartial observer of life as it really exists. In *Culture and Truth* (1989), Resaldo enumerates the stylistic ways in which an ethnographer creates this scientific ethos. Thus, we learn that an objectifying report of students, for instance, depends on a distanced, normalized mode of discourse, overextended assertions, and a view of a people as close to nature (and therefore primitive, in need of help) (92).

I would postulate that the rhetoric of composition's ethnographic teacher-research often does forward such a scientific view, rather than a phenomenological one. This rhetoric would reveal itself in discussing students as a homogeneous group rather than as individuals (as happens in William Coles' *The Plural I* where one student cannot be distinguished from another). Even our more recent research—which attempts to specify the axes of identity either accounted for or excluded—refers to our students as homogeneous in terms of their critical abilities, their ability with academic literacy, and so forth.

A Cartesian dualism would also reveal itself in a tendency to read students as "close" to their (racial, classed, or gendered) nature as opposed to critical, distanced, or in open conflict with such a nature. Finally, it could also be evidenced in our rhetoric of colonization in the name of "better" pastures—where the grass of academic literacy would lead to a better, healthier, (more democratic?) life for our nomadic students (who want to move from their homeland to better pastures anyway).

A person could take exception to these barely supported assertions, but still not fail to admit that scientism does—despite so much of our criticism—still structure much of composition's research scholarship. C.H. Knoblauch and Lil Brannon (1988) reveal our continued belief in this paradigm by documenting how funding for empirical, positivistic research still outnumbers funding for phenomenological research (20–21).

Even in presumed ethnographically oriented teacher-research, strands of empiricism run strong. I have noticed, for instance, that most NCTE teacher-research publications use lists and concrete elaborations of classroom practices as methods to support a claim. Most teacher research, whether presented in article or book form, tends to focus on classroom methods. A section on assessment, on paper assignments, on seating arrangements, on teaching research . . . such "how to" writing lends credence to the assertion of Knoblauch and Brannon that our field still finds itself "giving in" to the cultural capital of positivistic empiricism.

The real problem for composition's teacher-research lies with its overt claim to a phenomenological epistemology which, at first, it seems to put into practice, but combine this with textual bodies that still conform to a positivistic, empirical tradition and the overall effect creates a heroic narrative in which the teacher emerges as the primary arbiter of change. At a deeper level, these accounts narrate a teacher's subjective experience of this change more than they narrate the experiences of the anthropological "other"—the students in the process of learning or resisting learning. Composition scholars run up against the same representation problem experienced in anthropology: how can we claim to represent our students' experiences of change, growth, or resistance if our rhetoric emphasizes the teacher?

I suggest that in these narratives, the teacher, as narrator, fieldworker, and author, portrays herself as a kind of literary hero, in the Romantic tradition begun by William Wordsworth in his "Preface to the Lyrical Ballads" (1802). The literary heros of romanticism were primarily concerned with issues of subjectivity, of self-consciousness, and of how the self apprehends and articulates an experience of divinity, purity, or universal oneness. They internalized the notion of the social hero and turned it into a self-identity that could be arrived at through intense introspection of the self in relation to its natural environment.

For the teacher-researcher to define herself or himself as such a hero is not an inherent problem. After all, the romantics valued and gave cultural capital to the subjective introspection that can lead to positive change—on both individual and social levels. Such a self-identity is problematic, however, for a kind of research that professes to represent the "real" learning experience or situation of others, of students. When the hero trope becomes the primary means of structuring research, the plot, the angle of vision, and the lessons learned tend to focus on the teacher's perspectives, feelings, confusions, and revelations. The subjectivity of the teacher-researcher dominates the writing of the research, and therefore can—and I would argue—usually does—obscure the thoughts, feelings, and revelations (or lack thereof) of the students.

Moreover, such a trope can easily lead the teacher-researcher to focus on micro-economics instead of the structural features of the pedagogic scene— institutional constraints and/or the problems of race, class, or gender that often define so much of classroom interactions. Thus, it claims a phenomenological basis which, in practice, it does not have.

If teacher-researchers want to advocate a tolerance for ambiguity, which abandoning the scientific paradigm and embracing a narrative epistemology *should* do, and if they want a recognition and portrait of the complexity of learning, then they have to seek out tropes that allow for such representations. I want to urge teacher-researchers to focus on the ways in which agency shifts positions within what Kenneth Burke would call a *scene-act ratio*. To neglect these ratios does a disservice to our larger cause of forwarding a humanistic research methodology, because by nature, it also neglects the sociopolitical dynamics that shape any classroom scene.

The goal of this chapter has been to show that a crisis of authority and of representation exists in the ethnographic research of both anthropology and composition studies. Through an analysis of two tropes—the royal arrival and the old-fashioned castaway, I hope to have clarified a larger problem with composition's research: teacher-researchers tend to make themselves the focus of an ostensible study of "others" by using narrative design that contradicts the underlying philosophy of their research methodology.

I do not, at the moment, have solutions to this problem; however, I believe that perhaps we can create our authority in ways that do mirror the experiences of our students within the context of their learning situation. This may involve a better understanding of comparative rhetoric. It may also require us to study the various tropes and narrative structures that more accurately reflect our students' perceptions of their learning environment and experience. Perhaps some of this research is done under a different research genre—as the study of home literacy and its impact on schooling, for instance. Still, I want to emphasize that teacher-research needs to fulfill its imputed allegiance to a phenomenologically based research methodology. This will involve finding ways to portray scenes of learning with more accuracy and insight.

Notes

1. While there is neither time nor space for me to define *phenomenological epistemology*, understanding this "way of knowing" is crucial to understanding the premise for the following argument. I would point interested readers to Ruth Ray's *The Practice of Theory: Teacher-Research in Composition* (1993) for an explication of the phenomenological history of ethnography and teacher-research.

2. This movement also grew out of a concern, in the 1960s, with the discovered "bad marriage" between colonial ideology and anthropological practice and praxis. Scholars began to examine texts for their colonial subtexts and also to pose alternative ways of doing ethnography, ways that would better live up to the meaning of the word, "anthropology."

3. This, in fact, is James Clifford's main point in "On Ethnographic Allegory" where he argues that all ethnographies are allegories for the ethnographer's culture. They depend on narratological structures which our culture recognizes, accepts, and is moved by (99).

5

Covering One's Tracks
Respecting and Preserving Informant Anonymity

John Lofty and Richard Blot

After teaching in a Maine-island fishing community from 1978 to 1981, I (Lofty) returned in 1984 to begin fieldwork for an ethnographic study of the relationship between students' experiences of time and their reception of mainstream literacy. I was fortunate in that my former students and the adult members of the community allowed me to interview them about their values, beliefs, work, and literacy practices. Some but not all of the interviewees were very concerned, however, that both their identity and the location of their island should remain anonymous. Because the study focused on resistance to literacy and students-at-risk in a community that values its privacy, my agreement to respect anonymity was a critical condition for the study.

Other researchers on occasion, though, do identify by name the teachers, students, and schools about which they write. The concern to preserve informants' anonymity shown by anthropologists and sociologists now appears to be made less often by those pursuing one of the various kinds of qualitative research, including the growing community of educational and social-science ethnographers. Changing attitudes toward anonymity often indicate not breaches of confidence but reflect complex, conscious choices about what it means to conduct research and to write in a postmodern age (Marcus and Fischer).

The theoretical perspectives that shape our work situate observer and observed in a much closer I-thou relationship than in the past. We now view

For a careful reading of our arguments, many thanks to Ellen Westbrook. Our appreciation also for thoughtful revision suggestions to Mary Hallet and Pat Wilson. We are grateful to William Clohesy for his willingness to discuss our ideas in gestation and for his critical commentary.

as subjects those who once had been regarded more as objects of study in what Martin Buber (1970) refers to as an *I-it relationship*. Discussions in composition studies are informed by concepts of ownership, individualism, and community that privilege subjectivity (Elbow; Zemelman and Daniels). The identity of the voices we struggle to understand through our dialogue become, then, part of our own and thereby invite scrutiny. Questions of textual polyvocality, that is, of whose voice is speaking and being heard, also raise issues of identifying multiple authors. As members of an age that disseminates information widely, we simultaneously respect and grant personal privacy, yet in professional work increasingly we go public.

Epistemological shifts in how we make knowledge in postmodern research raise questions about the ethical codes that inform the practice of ethnography in diverse fields. The critical question we will address here is whether or not ethnographers name the subjects and locale of their work. Logistical and practical factors that determine whether a researcher ever can guarantee anonymity are critical to the efficacy of one's answer. We shall need, then, to look carefully at the pragmatic implications of the ethical question.

The need to discuss the ethics of how we report on ethnographic research makes at least two related assumptions. It assumes that writing about human-science research has actual or potential consequences for the lives of those with whom we create descriptions, narratives, and interpretations. It assumes also that to conduct research in an ethical framework requires us to protect and to consider the ethical rights of those we study. We need to consider both our stated intentions and the possible effects of what we do.

The position above is complicated, though, because how researchers define moral behavior in the field depends on the ethical theory or theories they endorse. In "Approaching ethical issues for qualitative researchers in education," Donna L. Deyhle and colleagues critique five theories of moral behavior synthesized from ethical positions framed by William F. May (1980):

1. The "teleological ethic," the end of enquiry as knowledge or truth, a good in itself;

2. The "utilitarian ethic," ethical behavior determined by cost benefit or the greatest good for the greatest number;

3. The "categorical imperative," ethical behavior determined by the principle of universals;

4. "Critical theory and advocacy," ethical research necessarily promoting the needs and interests of those being researched.

5. "Covenantal ethics," strongly influences the position we explore in this essay: May argues that the 1971 Principles of Professional Responsibility of the AAA (American Anthropological Association) moved in the direction of a covenantal ethic by acknowledging the specific obligations anthropologists incur "with colleagues, students, spouses, subjects, governments and groups with whom they do field work. . . . But the

statement makes clear that the researcher's primary responsibility is to those he [sic] studies. (Deyhle, 608)

In the current situation, researchers' ethical theories shape how they answer the question of whether to name their subjects and locale. We will address the question by examining the validity of the following position: Researchers should do all that they can to protect their subjects' rights to privacy and to ensure that informants cannot be traced by identifying information in the ethnographic descriptions. We will do so by using the structure of an argument. Lofty will present two arguments for the position; Blot will present the counterarguments to which Lofty will reply. Space limits our testing the proposition to only two rounds of argument. Rather than our assessing the balance of support for and against the position, we will leave that task for readers.

Lofty: My first argument is that to identify publicly the research community and its members has the potential to cause psychological harm to one's informants. For example, in 1984, I was invited to present my work at a regional conference attended by several Maine-island teachers. The organizer did not register my request not to identify the site of the research. After several hours of laboriously whiting out the island's name on the program, I began to wonder if my concern over anonymity was justified. Who would really know or care if the island was named?

When I read the session evaluations, an answer to the question came immediately. One evaluator commented harshly on what was interpreted as my critical judgments about "illiterate" people living in coastal Maine. An outsider, the person wrote, had shown a lack of respect for the language and culture of a community he neither knew nor understood. I was alarmed to read a major misinterpretation of what I had intended to convey about my students' resistance to the writing process in terms of their cultural time values and their strong preference to share ideas by talking rather than by writing.

Neither my intended meanings nor the reasonableness of the audience member's interpretation are the issue. Suppose that my efforts to conceal the research site had failed and that the perceived judgments of illiteracy had been reported back to the community, which to my knowledge did not occur. This person's perception could be received in several different ways. First, participants might be immediately hurt. By report, students could learn that they had been described publicly as "illiterates" who resisted the best efforts of those who taught them to read and write. Students likely would respond to "illiterate" in terms of its highly charged pejorative meanings—"having little or no education, unable to read and write, and violating approved patterns of speaking or writing" (*Webster's Collegiate Dictionary*).

My former colleagues at the conference would be charged with having failed to impart what we regard as the most basic set of verbal skills. To apply the term *illiteracy* to late twentieth-century North Americans is to associate their verbal abilities with those living in so-called *third-world countries* in which illiteracy has yet to be "eradicated." The extent to which people internalize the negative evaluations of others would vary by individual and by the status of the evaluator. Arguably, some community members would dismiss a judgment by one more person from "away" who failed to understand and appreciate local language uses.

The effects on the researcher and on future research is also a concern. Once a descriptor such as "illiterate" has been attached publicly to a community, erasing it would be difficult. We can imagine the researcher explaining, "No, I never used the word illiterate. I said that people valued and therefore used talk more than writing," an observation applicable to many communities. Such heartfelt explanations likely would be heard at best as apologies because of the reactive context that elicited them.

Once the damage of culturally elite judgments is done, the researcher's attempts to sustain access to families and to record further conversations is likely to be difficult. Worse yet, because the ethnographer's subjects now have been publicly objectified in negative ways, participants will regard the researcher as having betrayed the informant's trust and understanding. Although one can always find another research site, our professional friends' respect and trust is now probably lost. Whether such a situation is likely to occur in comparable cases does not affect an argument designed to explore possible consequences. Neither does providing one example prove an argument; it invites readers, though, to consider the kinds of harm that identifying subjects and site can cause and have caused in the past and likely will cause in the future.

We need next to distinguish between the claim that to maintain confidentiality is an ethical responsibility and the practical question of whether one can cover one's tracks from the research site through to the writing. For me, the question is a logistical one that does not affect the ethical terms of the position. When I have raised the issue, colleagues have observed that preserving the anonymity of the island is likely to be very difficult. By extension, then, if for circumstantial reasons it appears unlikely that privacy can be maintained, the researcher is relieved somehow of the ethical responsibility to try.

Pragmatic solutions to ethical dilemmas can be persuasive. Our starting premise and attendant responsibility to do all that we can to avoid harming subjects physically or psychologically prohibits such solutions. The ease or difficulty of respecting this condition does not change the ethical value of the premise itself. If we knew with reasonable certainty from the outset that we could not ensure privacy, then I would argue we should consider quitting a project.

Blot: As a cultural anthropologist, I reply to Lofty's argument based on my own fieldwork experiences and by drawing on recent documents of the Commission to Review the AAA (American Anthropological Association) Statements on Ethics. I offer my counterarguments as brief commentary not as attempts at resolution.

The first point to address is Lofty's concern that we protect individuals and the community by offering anonymity to both. One implication of his argument is that the anonymity offered to individual research subjects may be compromised if we cannot ensure anonymity to the community. Good reasons may exist, though, to separate respect for an individual's anonymity from attempts to ensure anonymity for a community. A researcher documenting the struggles of a native-American community to assert its identity in the face of government nonrecognition would do well to support the community's claim, while simultaneously ensuring the anonymity of individual informants (Collins). We need to ask: Under what conditions does a group need to remain anonymous? Such an enquiry raises further questions: How would the researcher offer anonymity to a community? Who speaks for the community? The Commission considering the "responsibilities [of researchers] to peoples and cultures studied," further complicates our task:

> Who determines what is in the best interests of the people studied? Most communities will not be of one mind as to what is in their best interests, and it seems paternalistic, if not presumptuous, to expect an anthropological researcher to make that judgment for someone else.
>
> Who decides who has access to information? Information is potential power and can be used to effect change. When change occurs, there usually are winners and losers. If the person providing the information decides in favor of recognition or chooses to use the information for his or her own ends, an anthropological researcher's ability to pick and choose winners and losers (the general welfare) is diluted, if it ever existed.
>
> Do all groups studied by anthropologists deserve efforts to promote the group's general welfare? It would seem not (i.e., hate groups, terrorists, drug cartels, etc.). . ... (AAA Final Report, 14)

Certainly anyone engaged in or contemplating ethnographic research would not be hard-pressed for examples, real or imagined, of potential harm to those among whom one does research. Social science literature is filled with cases, some of which are notorious (Boas; Wolf and Jorgensen).

The question, after all, is not about the possibility of harm to subjects. That possibility is always and everywhere present. Its ubiquity is recognized clearly, for example, in the ethical precepts presented by the AAA: "To do no harm or wrong, understanding that the development of knowledge can lead to change which may be positive or negative for the people or animals worked with or studied" (Draft AAA Code of Ethics, 15). Further, the code of ethics stipulates that: "Anthropological researchers must determine in advance whether their hosts/providers of information wish to remain anonymous or receive recognition, and make every effort to comply with their wishes" (*Ibid.*, 15). Our concern here, rather, is whether to ensure the anonymity of the subjects is necessary to afford protection from potential harm, and whether it is the best or the only way to do so. Further, one must ask whether it is the researcher alone who has the responsibility and the means to do so.

Let us consider the penultimate point first. Lofty, in his statement of the proposition, "Researchers should do all they can, not only to protect the subjects' rights to privacy, but also to ensure that informants cannot be traced by identifying information in the ethnographic descriptions," has linked subjects' right to privacy with subjects' anonymity. Is the only way to protect privacy to ensure anonymity? Clearly, this is not so. A party named in a lawsuit is not anonymous, but being named does not violate the person's rights to privacy. Instead, it sets up a special area of privacy; the nature and content of communication between client and attorney are protected. Similar cases are well-known: doctor and patient, confessor and penitent. Although we may conclude that any necessary link between anonymity and privacy is unwarranted, we still would want to ask whether the relationship between ethnographer and subject constitutes such a special case.

To answer this we need to say something about ethnography. The purpose of ethnography is to describe sociocultural phenomena and the means by which they are created and sustained by real actors performing real events. The products of ethnography are not fictions but instead result from a process carried out in a real community of very real people. Because we are concerned with actual people, ethical obligations loom large. In this context, when providing factual descriptions, we would need to determine how much anonymity is necessary to protect the subjects and how much is necessary to ensure the factual nature of the description. If we camouflage our subjects to such a degree that we render them nonentities in real situations, what aspect of the social world have we described? With what accuracy? If our descriptions create nonentities, we have reduced subjects to objects. One is reminded of the distinguished anthropologist Stanley Diamond's (1974) warning to fieldworkers: "The anthropologist, confronting the native, must constantly struggle against reducing both himself and the other to ciphers in a scientific experiment" (80). That many ethnographers, especially those engaged in education research in their own communities, no longer feel the confrontational encounter of self with others in their fieldwork gives Diamond's warning more rather than less import.

Lofty: To allow space for the second argument, my reply must be brief. Blot first distinguishes between the ethnographer's efforts to offer anonymity to the community and to individuals and finds good reasons to separate them. To act based on whether ethnographers choose paternalism or enlightened regard for a community's right to determine its own spokespeople is to determine our ethics by what we deem practical. If a community or its school is named, then the informants within likely can and eventually will be identified. Conversely, communities can be identified if we name individuals. Blot's question, though, "How would the researcher offer anonymity to a community?" underscores the problem of making assurances that state a researcher's intent but cannot be taken as a guarantee, for example, because other subjects may publicly identify themselves.

Blot's quote from the AAA Code of Ethics addresses usefully the responsibilities of researchers to peoples and cultures studied. The AAA recognizes that both harm and good result from publishing ethnographic descriptions. If, then, we regard our subjects' welfare of primary importance, the researcher always must ask the likelihood of the research's placing subjects at risks they otherwise would not have assumed or encountered. Attempting to ensure the anonymity of the subject, then, becomes an essential but not necessarily a sufficient condition "to afford protection from potential harm." Anonymity is one of several necessary conditions; Blot, however, suggests that its necessity is contingent.

His analogy of the relationship between an ethnographer and a subject, and a client and an attorney, is problematic. For litigation, accuser and accused both must be publicly identified. In contrast, for ethnographers to conduct research, subjects do not need to be identified. Although both client and subject enjoy rights to privacy and to silence, the subject has volunteered to provide information, whereas a client may well be called on to testify. If subjects make statements about their opinions, beliefs, and values but subsequently are identified publicly, then it is hard to see that privacy of opinion has been preserved. Once again, however, anonymity is a necessary, but not necessarily a sufficient, condition for privacy.

My second argument is that if we ensure our informants of their anonymity, then as researchers we are maximally free to report what we find. If we name our research sites and/or informants, we are limited in our ability to describe fully, for example, teaching practices that we regard as problematic or that we see as abusing students' rights. To present perspectives on instruction critical of a teacher or a teaching style could place students at risk.

At first sight, this might appear to be a practical rather than an ethical issue; lack of anonymity, I will argue, can constrain ethical action. Deyhle and colleagues (1992) argue that the "[E]thical treatment of the data requires that the researcher be scrupulously honest in seeking out negative cases, and alternate explanations of phenomena" (636). If subjects are identified by name and by school, then fully disclosing our findings potentially places much more at risk than does revealing findings about anonymous people and their communities.

My own work has described the effects of institutional time on students' abilities and motivations to write. My purpose has been to critique time values inherited from nineteenth-century industrial practices. Consequently, although I am holding neither individual teachers nor school systems responsible, a reader might infer some responsibility because other pedagogic practices or a refusal to participate in the system were not chosen. Anonymity makes it possible to describe school and community without undue fear of a criticism being leveled against a specific teacher or school system.

The two examples below show how naming one's subjects can affect the nature of what does and does not get represented. A researcher has been involved for several years now in working with students and teachers in a large, inner-city school district. Published research identifies school district and teachers by name. When I asked the researcher about how problematic practices were reported, the answer was that nothing negative or critical was ever written about the teachers or the school. Only positive portraits have been published.

A second example. A researcher studying the dynamics among members of a creative writing group felt unable to describe the interpersonal tensions that arose because the group was identified. The tensions occurred, in part, because the writers did not all share the same assumptions about responding to fiction and because the group's leader had chosen not to open discussion about their differences in theoretical positions. Once the group was identified, exploring the effects of the differences in relation to the group dynamic became most difficult. Had the group remained anonymous, the researcher would have been freer to write about tensions which could only be talked about privately. The researcher's own participant-observer relationship with the group also could have been explored.

We need also to consider the relationship between the range of purposes of ethnographic research—from its inception to publication—and the issue of anonymity. Mike Rose (1995), who in *Possible Lives* names his teachers and schools, rightly observes that national debates on education often present only "despairing" and "dismissive" assessments of public schooling. He argues that "[W]e are in desperate need of rich, detailed images of possibility" (4), which his inspiring vignettes of classroom life certainly provide. If our descriptions render only the positive, though, then we risk compromising what I take as our professional responsibility to describe what we find including negative cases. Conversely, we are under the same responsibility to report positive features when we are studying what is dysfunctional in educational systems. Not surprisingly perhaps, what we believe to be effective and limiting practices often coexist in the same school, and in the same classroom.

Blot: When anonymity is offered to subjects, and accepted, the subjects have ceded any power they have had, however little, to influence the ethnographer's description. This supports Lofty's contention that to provide anonymity frees the researcher to report what has been found. But it raises the issue of whose voices are being represented and who controls what they say. Does the offer of anonymity, as part of the covenant between researcher and subjects, preclude the possibility that subjects may retain some degree of influence, even veto power, over what is reported?

An even more pertinent issue regards the degree of shared understanding. To what extent must research subjects grasp the ethnographer's intentions and the purpose of the project in order to participate in a covenant? To argue that subjects must have a complete understanding, for example, of Lofty's own research purposes and goals, begs the question as to what counts as "complete." Further, in most ethnographic studies, the questions to be asked emerge in the course of the study. Therefore, these could not be discussed fully with subjects at the outset of the study.

The degree of shared understanding possible will be related to the exigencies of the field situation. Certainly, work with children, to take one example, presents interesting ethical as well as methodological challenges. The temptation, however, is to answer whatever questions arise around the issue situationally; that would seem to be the source of many of the ethical dilemmas of fieldwork. What is more difficult to develop, even though desperately required, is a normative basis for ethical relations in ethnography.

This would entail a full-scale investigation of the nature of anthropological knowledge to determine if any basis for norms exists. This is not a question of methodology, but one of the epistemological foundations of ethical principles. Until this work is carried forward, before we embark upon fieldwork we do well to remember Barnes' (1977) words: "The question is not how refracting objects of research can be manipulated without trauma but rather how negotiations can be effectively concluded with other human beings so that the social scientist achieves his research aims without violating the aims and expectations of the citizens he studies" (7).

Many ethnographers in the postmodern world believe themselves to be engaged in rendering, in concert with their subjects, interpretations of sociocultural phenomena that adequately represent the struggle of multiple voices to create the meanings of any communication. Thus, any ethnographic description is an interpretive representation of an event, series of events, even a whole way of life, a representation that opens a pathway for readers into these events or way of life. If the subjects of any enquiry are rendered completely anonymous, whose voices are we hearing? The description provided by the now univocal ethnographer who chooses which voices to incorporate in the product and in what ways to use and make them accessible to the reader is most important here. What judgments can be made as to the commensurability of this or that ethnographic account to his or her own situation? In what ways does it resonate and how is he or she to judge its degree of resonance?

The relationship between ethnographer and subjects for research includes an area of interaction, of interpretive acts, closed to the reader, because it is not rendered as part of the description. This protects the subjects, but it also may "protect" the ethnographer. It forces us also to the question, which is beyond the scope of this essay, regarding the responsibility of the ethnographer to the research community for whom we write. We need only to ask, does the research community allow for a special relationship between ethnographer and subject to be created because it is an essential condition of ethnography?

Here we uncover the difference between the attorney-client relationship and that of the ethnographer to the subjects of research. When protecting communication between attorney and client, the courts do not expect that the content of that communication will be publicly revealed. In fact, the ability of the attorney to represent the client may depend on the assurance that information remain hidden. Ethnographers, however, cannot honestly tell their research subjects that they will keep the information provided hidden from public view precisely because the general purpose of the research is to increase social-science knowledge. The expectation is that information gained will be shared, and accurate representation depends on it. This does not mean, though, that the individual's proper name be revealed.

Lofty: Blot pointedly observes that "when anonymity is offered to subjects, and accepted, the subjects have ceded any power, however little they might have had to influence the ethnographer's description." He rightly asks whether subjects also have forfeited any "veto power" over what gets reported. Whether they do so depends on the ethnographer's behavior and specifically the ways and extents to which we involve our subjects in the research and writing.

I have argued above that one ethical imperative of research is to report what one finds especially when findings are mixed or reports conflict. When a subject has accepted anonymity, the already existing responsibility to disclose fully is only deepened. To ensure that subjects' perspectives are accurately rendered, descriptions ideally will be shared during the writing stage. Accuracy of statement can be checked, further information or qualifications can be included and any differences in interpretation as to what descriptions might mean can be acknowledged. Blot's counter underscores key ethical concerns with clear implications for ethnographic writing. His second concern regarding subjects' comprehension of validity is hard to dispute: an informant might well not fully understand a researchers' agenda and questions.

The elementary school–age children with whom I worked could not have understood "completely" either the experiential concepts of time that I was exploring, nor could they have visualized the relationship between the questions I was asking and the book I would finally write; as author, neither could I. High school students and adults, too, probably did not comprehend fully my interests in the relations between time and identity and their uses of language. Although Blot is right in arguing that to establish a covenantal relationship with subjects presupposes degrees of shared understanding, that an understanding might be only partial does not remove the need to respect covenants and subjects' anonymity.

The second aspect of Blot's counter is equally thorny to refute; he observes that ethnographers' questions evolve over time. When I began the interviews in 1984, my understanding of time was simpler and more limited than was expressed in subsequent questions of 1986 and 1990. Time for writing and reflection on answers given, and further reading, too, prompted me to evolve questions that targeted more closely the complexity of what I had set out to understand; the target had shifted. Communities do not hold still as we attempt to portray them. Given, then, the strong possibility that subjects and researcher only partially will share their understanding of a project and its possible impact on a community and that questions likely will evolve, the researcher is responsible for honoring the trust that the covenant establishes—a value judgment supported by Barnes' quote.

The final part of Blot's counter addresses the issue of what it might mean for us to do ethnography in a postmodern world and "to be engaged in rendering in concert with their subjects, interpretations of sociocultural phenomena." His argument rests on the premise that for an ethnographer to represent "events" or "a whole way of life," the subjects portrayed must be identifiable, a condition essential for readers to determine the degree of "resonance" or "commensurability" between an ethnographic account and the subjects' "[historical] situation."

His concern that readers determine for themselves the value and credibility of a study is an important one to establish; the issue, though, is how we do that. Even if readers were able to go into the community and interview the same people using identical questions, the ensuing conversations, descriptions, and interpretations likely would be both similar and different. The reason for disparity is predictable, given the paradigm of qualitative research; we cannot verify findings by duplicating fieldwork as we might for experimental research. To know the names of community and individuals likely will not benefit the reader—beyond satisfying understandable curiosity—but identifications potentially can and have harmed subjects, as Blot acknowledges. Consequently, ensuring anonymity loses nothing central to the representations, but it may well protect subjects from harm.

Blot: If indeed our responsibility to research subjects is based on "covenant ethics," we need to enquire into the nature of that covenant. We may begin by arguing that one necessary aspect of any covenant is reciprocity. The encounter between ethnographer and the subjects of research often is understood as obligating the ethnographer to reciprocate. The subjects provide access to the events and practices of their everyday lives. In return, the ethnographer is called upon, many would argue, to provide something of value in return. This is not as simple or as straightforward as one might expect. Diamond (1974) tells us that during his fieldwork among the Anaguta, one of his key informants

> was charged by a younger man of his lineage with betraying tribal secrets and was publicly slapped [a great insult]. I was being given rituals, part of the living body of the people, it was said, and it was true as everyone knew, for I had explained my mission to all who would listen. Even the subtler aspects of the charges were true. For what sacred thing was given the Anaguta in return for what they were giving me? What could I give them? (71)

The covenant as the basis for ethical relations between ethnographer and research subjects may be inadequate if we understand the notion of covenant to imply either shared power or shared understanding. That parties to any covenant need not be equally powerful nor even to share power should be obvious. We need take only one example: the relative position of researcher, teacher, student, school principal, school-board member and so forth amply demonstrate the inequities of power in educational institutions.

Lofty: Blot's claim that reciprocity is an entailment of covenant breaks ethical ground beyond the position that we have argued above and raises a further question about how we handle anonymity. Is the ethnographer under any kind of reciprocal obligation to support publicly the professional lives of those who have made the study possible? Letters of support or recommendation— which on occasion I write—could link researcher, subject, and site.

The ethnographer, whether working in schools, project housing, or corporate America, inhabits a critical position: he or she can give voice to those who have power and influence and can give voice to the disenfranchised from whom we stand to learn a great deal about ourselves in relation to others. In most cases, even if reciprocal exchanges could be orchestrated, any expectation of reciprocity would limit the spirit and intent of why ethnographers make descriptions. And as Blot points out above, covenants enable people differently situated along the continuum of power to work together, to share understanding and to be represented in respectful ways.

Blot and Lofty: Our final comments ask readers to think broadly and carefully about the purposes of representation. The ethical entailments of serving those purposes obligates us to address responsibly the issue of subjects' anonymity. Although ethnographers seek to present subjects and not objects or nonentities, with few exceptions, the ethnographer's purpose is not to represent the individual subject as a particular person. Rather the purpose is to describe an individual as representative of a social role and the cultural ways of a people. Although the individuals represented in an ethnography are real people in their historical circumstances, their individual identities are less important to readers than accurate representations of the cultural configurations that "define" them. Readers now can assess for themselves the balance of evidence for and against the position that we have argued. We hope also that readers will see the kinds and complexity of issues that testing the claim for preserving subjects' anonymity raises for ethnographic research.

6

Materialist Methods
Ethnography and Transformation
Gwen Gorzelsky

"I think if you knew you were going to write this when you came over to talk to us that afternoon, you should have told us!" declared angular, fortyish Paula, her eyes smoldering, her raspy voice deepening.

I looked into her eyes and replied, "I didn't. I just came over to talk and then went home and thought, 'What a great conversation!'" As I sat at Paula's kitchen table between her and Renee, I was acutely conscious of my outsider status—in a neighborhood where such distinctions can determine one's safety, I was from across town, younger, childless, aspiring professional, and white. Facing the two women's anger on their turf, I was grateful I could truthfully repeat, "If I'd known I was going to write about it, I'd have told you."

Paula had invited me, and I knew I was physically safe. My intestinal fluttering sprang from the recognition that these women, whom I liked and respected, whom I hoped to join in their efforts to reform their community and open possibilities for its children, clearly believed I had betrayed them. I assured them that I would not publish the essay we had discussed, the one I had grounded partly in a generative conversation with them. We talked, moving from the essay to their neighborhood work, to each of our lives. When Paula offered tea and lunch, I felt some of the tension flow out of my body. I listened to their plans for the project. We arranged that I would help to write a funding proposal letter later in the spring. Each of them shook my hand before we dispersed on separate errands.

My sincere thanks to Jonathan Arac, David Bartholomae, Joyce Baskins, Stephen Carr, Eric Clarke, Cristina Kirklighter, Geeta Kothari, Elenore Long, Joseph Moxley, Julia Sawyer, and Cloe Vincent for their comments and suggestions on this paper. They are responsible for many of its strengths and none of its weaknesses.

When I had taken copies of the essay to Paula and Renee and asked them to sign publishing permissions, I had butterflies of anxiety. Would Renee resent the depictions of her spelling anxiety? Would Paula dislike the characterization of her long-limbed frame? There were larger issues—my portrayal of Renee's recovery and rebuilding after years as the addicted girlfriend of another neighborhood's drug kingpin, to start. But as a participant in our inner-city community center's self-development through writing project, she had discussed those events openly and used the project as part of her process of self-revision. I did not think Renee would object to the paper's limited disclosure of her history.

She did not. At least, not in that way.

Like life, ethnography is a messy practice, full of contradictory truths. This messiness makes it both difficult to theorize cogently and potentially unproductive. My paper begins to think through ethnography's inevitably compromised and compromising aspects, its problems and possibilities.

My opening discussion of materialist dialectics via Marx, Louis Althusser, and Richard Johnson describes empirical work—including ethnography—as a practice that inevitably produces subjective knowledge. I argue that because any knowledge must contend with others' alternative representations, the real still shapes knowledge and the conceptual frameworks producing it. Finally, I suggest that disenfranchised ways of seeing might use ethnography to pressure the academic frameworks that generate it. To explore how this pressure might operate, my second section examines the question of ethnography's legitimation and (literary) form as discussed by George Marcus (1982), Barbara Myerhoff and Jay Ruby (1982), and Paul Rabinow (1982) and by discussing Gayatri Spivak's (1988) work on similar problems in the practice of history. I conclude the section by suggesting that as a quasi-literary form, ethnography may afford a vehicle for both cathexis—emotional-intellectual investments—and for pressuring revisions of dominant conceptual frameworks. In the third section, I use Spivak's revision of important Marxist categories to argue that ethnography must address the problems of ideology, cathexis, and consciousness in imagining its own role in sociopolitical transformation. The final section builds on my reading of Spivak to argue that a literary ethnography would broaden the possibilities for working toward ethical representation. By sketching my current ethnographic project's efforts to enact this approach and describing that project's possibilities and limits, I lay out some of the problems and potential involved in such a revision of ethnographic practice.

Materialist Dialectics:
Conceptual Frameworks' Struggle

"This is all just gossip that we was talkin'," Renee insisted of the conversation I had depicted. "I mean, it's true, but it's still gossip." Her partially straightened, shoulder-length ponytail bobbed for emphasis.

My mind flashed to the account of her effort, with Paula, to scour their public housing unit of crack dealing, public drinking and marijuana smoking, loud profanity, and violence. I recalled the paper's portrayal of their plans, of the work they'd already shouldered, of their concern for the unit's kids, who were frequently endangered by drive-by shootings. Still listening, I groped for an understanding of what "gossip" meant here.

Her long, professionally manicured nails drawn together in a point as her hand punctuated each sentence with a forward thrust, Renee explained. Her rapport with fellow-residents was important, she emphasized. If the plan to clean up the housing unit was to work, she could not look stuck up or holier-than-thou, particularly as someone who had lived the street life herself.

"If they read this," she concluded, "these people will feel betrayed."

As attempts to grasp the materiality of situations and events, this essay's depictions of Renee and Paula are, of course, fraught with the problems of representation. One problem is the difficulty in distinguishing the representer's— my—conceptual framework(s) from the reality being represented. Marx's *Grundrisse* (1859) takes up this issue, as do two of its critiques, Louis Althusser's "On the Materialist Dialectic" (1969) and Richard Johnson's "Reading for the Best Marx: History-Writing and Historical Abstraction" (1982). Despite differences between Althusser and Johnson on how the materialist dialectic works, both emphasize Marx's point that the observers' perspective inevitably shapes the knowledge they produce. Each takes up the problem of how the conceptual frameworks grounding any observer's perspective shape such knowledge. And both demonstrate Marx's use of critique to grapple with the problem of perspective. By critiquing the abstractions of a given conceptual framework—for instance, ethnography's separate categories of ethnographer and ethnographic subject—Marx deepens that framework's access to reality. He makes its abstractions more complex and concrete. Marx, Althusser, and Johnson argue that the real produces contradictions that pressure and reshape conceptual frameworks' abstract categories by means of critique. The contradictions that emerge in the practice of ethnography, then, might produce a useful critique of its categories.

But in *The Grundrisse*, Marx builds his critique and methodology by introducing his *own* data into the conceptual framework he critiques. Johnson and Althusser hold that the real produces contradictions and that these contradictions pressure and reshape theory and its abstract categories. They each argue that critique drives this process. Yet what neither Marx, in the *Grundrisse* passage, nor his explicators acknowledge is that these contradictions emerging from the real are *representations*, representations structured and produced by conceptual frameworks.

I am suggesting that the only way the real can pressure a theory or conceptual framework—and thus reshape it—is through the mediation of the same (or another) conceptual framework. Alternative ways of understanding the world and producing knowledge drive the process that makes our abstract

categories more concrete and complex. Ethnography seeks to act as critique
does in Marx's terms—it seeks to revise our own conceptual framework(s) by
introducing alternative ways of understanding the world, by putting conceptual
frameworks in dialogue and tension with one another.

Yet, no matter how effectively the earlier version of this chapter
represented tensions in my portrayal of the conversation with Paula and Renee,
my conceptual frameworks inevitably structured its representations. No matter
how rigorously that essay strove to put their many-sided conversation in tension
with the conceptual frameworks grounding the paper, its representation
remained an amputated limb, a portrayal cut off from its source and thus unable
to represent that source's range of responses. And yet working to produce a
representation that brings those discourses into negotiation is the only way that
I can see at this point to push on, to make more concrete and complex my own
conceptual frameworks.

Ethnography: Legitimation and Literary Form

Renee's rapport meant even more than the success or failure of the reform
project she and Paula had undertaken, I began to realize.

"We have to live with these people," Paula insisted, her open-palmed hand
cutting the air in front of her in a downward swipe. The network of dealers was
not going to disappear, and neither Paula nor Renee imagined that these
adolescent boys and young men would be swept en masse into the legal
system's maw. Nor did they want such results. Cleaning up the housing project
meant something different.

Gradually, I began to glimpse the parameters of another ethical framework. If the dealers—many of the neighborhood's young men—would take
their business, their forties and blunts,[1] their loud profanity away from the
unit's public spaces, its playground, and especially its kids, their behavior
would be tolerated. No calls to the local police task force. No reports to
officials. No informing. Certainly no published texts exposing them.

"They're good kids. They're our kids," said Paula of the dealers she had
earlier castigated.

"That's right," added Renee. "They listen to us. They respect us."

The problem for ethnographers, as I have outlined via Marx, Althusser,
and Johnson, is how to acknowledge and account for the ways in which our
conceptual frameworks inevitably shape the knowledge we produce and yet
still claim that this knowledge improves our access to the real. In this section,
I will examine that question in terms of narrative and literary form to explore
how disenfranchised conceptual frameworks might use ethnography to
pressure and revise the frameworks that generate it.

The problem of ethnography's legitimation emerges specifically through its
construction as narrative. Narrative forms point inherently, though not always
self-consciously, to their own perspectival, subjective nature and to their status as

representations. Thus, ethnography must address the question of its legitimation via narrative and rhetoric. If one sees ethnography as a potential site of struggle among conceptual frameworks' representations, its legitimation problem is, simultaneously, the source of its power to deepen our access to the real.

Ethnography's narrative form raises other possibilities as well. Gayatri Spivak's "Can the Subaltern Speak?" (1988) illustrates historical representations' tendency to freeze their subjects' consciousnesses and actions into static models or objects of investigation. This danger, of course, besets ethnographic narratives as well. Spivak posits another possibility, namely that historical narratives might provide opportunities for cathexis—for readers to form emotional-intellectual investments. Such cathexis, as I understand Spivak, can enable interventionist rewriting of the social text by helping to reconstruct historical (and, I'd suggest, ethnographic) subjects' consciousnesses around what she calls *counterhegemonic ideology.*

Understanding ethnography as a literary form highlights its potential to prompt cathexis. Barbara Myerhoff and Jay Ruby, in their introduction to *A Crack in the Mirror: Reflexive Perspectives in Anthropology* (1982), discuss ethnography as a literary genre, as do the essays by George Marcus and Paul Rabinow in the same volume (23). These positions support a reading of ethnography as *both* aesthetic and "factual." I would suggest that an ethnography that self-consciously combines "rational" analysis with aesthetic elements and structure might offer what Rabinow calls "new modes of relating to the social world" (185). It might foster readers' cathexis.[2]

Yet the investments into which cathexis taps differ from one audience to another. My earlier paper sought to prompt literacy workers' investments in work that would connect processes of self-revision with those of community renewal. But because even strenuous ethnographic practice can provide at best a subjective representation of both the processes and the individuals engaged in them, Paula's and Renee's responses diverged sharply from those of my academic readers. I was forced to confront the limits of my ethnographic practice.

In this paper, I am still working for cathexis. But this time I am seeking to prompt academic readers' investment in a revised practice of ethnography.

Ethnography: Ideology, Cathexis, and Consciousness

"If I ever saw this in print, I'd know who it was about," said Renee of my essay. "I mean, not right away. But I'd read it three, four, five times. And I'd know. Ohhh," she parodied, *"that's* who that is."

"It's all there," agreed Paula. "People would know who we are even though you changed the names." Their own family members, especially the kids who lived in the apartment complex, wouldn't be safe from retribution. "And these people," she said of the dealers, "they respect us because we *don't* do things like this. And they *do* read, they know what's in the paper. If we do this, we won't be safe."

"That's right," Renee said. "Because anyone who lives here would know who these people are that we're talking about," she added, referring to the paper's version of their conversation. "They'll think we betrayed them, that we went behind their backs."

"Of course I won't use it," I assured them, gesturing toward the copies of the essay on the kitchen table. I'd explained that the book including my paper was aimed at readers pursuing teaching degrees, thinking that the narrow circulation of most academic, rather than commercial, texts made its likelihood of reaching this urban neighborhood slim. But I knew the question was moot. The possible consequences for Renee, Paula, and their families were too serious even for the infinitesimal risk that a copy would, by way of the community center where I worked, make its way into the hands of someone from this crosstown neighborhood.

Focusing on ethnography's potential to spark cathexis can in fact begin a critique, a revision, of both ethnography's categories and Marxism's conceptual framework. This section will use Spivak's revision of that framework to argue that ethnography must engage with the problems of ideology, cathexis, and consciousness to imagine its own role in sociopolitical transformation.

I read Chapter five, "Limits and Openings of Marx in Derrida," (1993) of Spivak's *Outside in the Teaching Machine* as, in part, an extension of her work in "Can the Subaltern Speak?" The chapter critiques Marx's slippery use of the term *social* in theorizing class consciousness, ideology, and transformation. In Spivak's reading, systemic socialism fails because Marx does not adequately address the problem of ideology as it shapes experience into meaning and, by extension, does not address the emotional-intellectual investments that construct people's consciousnesses and day-to-day practices. Thus, Spivak's explanation of materialist methodology emphasizes attending to, negotiating with, the ideological understandings of experience and the processes of cathexis that generate them. In "Can the subaltern speak?," she stresses the need "to learn to speak to (rather than listen to or speak for) the historically muted subject of the subaltern woman." Thus, she highlights the need for materialist methodologies—and, of course, ethnography is one—to negotiate with such ideological understandings and the consciousnesses they produce (Spivak, 1988, 295). Finally, when she claims that systemic socialism fails because it sidesteps these issues, Spivak emphasizes that to think transition—transformation—one must grapple with schematic ideology, cathexis, and consciousness.

To imagine—and craft—an ethnography that might support Renee and Paula in their efforts at transformative work, an ethnography in which they (as well as academic and literacy-oriented readers) could invest, means struggling with these questions. The depiction of my conversation with them points to the complexity of the effort to "speak to" others: ideology functions as one of the mechanisms that construct us, but its workings are not simple or predetermined. And ideologies—of empirical access to reality, of the transformative power of knowledge—undergird my depiction just as they do Paula's and Renee's discourse.

Ethnography: Limits and (Im)Possibilities

But there is no Renee. There is no Paula. These are not pseudonyms coupled with a blurring of identifying details. In that sense, this paper is a failed ethnography. Its characters are composites. I have culled gestures, physical characteristics, and dialogue from multiple sources, people whom I have encountered through the community center. The conversation portrayed is a fiction that nonetheless bears some relation to the interaction that inspired it. The story of the ghost paper behind this one, the paper I promised not to publish and will not, is "true," as is this paper's explanation of why I cannot.

"You can't just alter the identifying information?" a colleague asked me after I recounted the incident to him. When I said no, explaining that depicting the substance of my characters' background and work in a community center program and their neighborhood could identify them, he asked, "So what happens to any empirical weight the paper had?"

Using ethnography to represent others' consciousnesses as well as to speak to and work with them is a vexed project. Spivak's *Teaching Machine's* (1993) Chapter five illustrates that any attempt at ethical representation must continually strive to formulate itself in terms of its subjects' ethics while recognizing the impossibility of fully achieving such formulation, recognizing that representation is inevitably a betrayal and an endless project. Each representation, she demonstrates, presupposes its own silent other, of and for which a further representation must be produced. At the same time, such representations must work to revise the conceptual frameworks—like empiricism and Marxism—that underlie their portrayals.

Yet while Spivak argues for narratives in which subalterns can invest, she does not address the question of how subalterns might use revised ideological investments and consciousnesses to transform their reality. The question of how its subjects might reverse the channel of power that operates through knowledge production is crucial.

With Spivak, then, I am arguing for an ethnography composed so that its subjects might also be its readers, an ethnography whose content is negotiated with its subjects. The challenge is to craft an ethnography whose representations are not only accessible to its ethnographic subjects and their emotional-intellectual investments but also negotiated with those subjects. Such ethnographic representations would thus work toward not only the ethnographer's ends but also toward the ethnographic subjects' ends. As a substantive revision prompted by a conversation with my ethnographic subjects, this paper moves only part way toward such work. I am extending Spivak's position to argue for practices that this paper does not enact: first, affording space, within the context of an ethnography's positioning as "legitimated" knowledge, for its subjects to craft their self-representations and second, negotiating the ethnographic work's representations with its subjects. In effect, the practice of ethnography—my interactions with the people who inspired the characters Paula and Renee—has prompted me to critique ethnography by suggesting a revision of its categories of ethnographer and ethnographic subjects.

A self-consciously literary ethnography could enable such work. To begin, writers could deliberately craft such narratives to foster cathexis and to enact a negotiation among ethnographers' and ethnographic subjects' conceptual frameworks. A literary approach could also afford ethnographer and ethnographic subjects the flexibility to negotiate the ethnography's content and structure. Finally, it would provide a wider range of formal possibilities, and that range could broaden the text's means to work toward ethical representation. For instance, a structure that juxtaposes historical and ethnographic components could work against freezing representations of others into static objects of investigation and could offer a way to speak to ethnographic subjects' ideologies and investments. This kind of literary ethnography might fundamentally transform our notions of what empirical weight means.

In my current ethnographic study, I am working to tap some of these possibilities. The study will include pieces written by my community center colleagues, both academic and nonacademic. By interspersing their chapters with my own, I hope to shape an ethnography that negotiates my ends with theirs. Because the study has shifted its focus away from participants in community center programs and toward the unfolding of one project, a joint endeavor involving community activists and academics, it will be largely autoethnographic. This move locates ethnographic inquiry in the processes and problems of building a shared agenda and project among academics from very different subdisciplines and community activists from very different backgrounds. Of course, it simultaneously produces a tension between the autoethnographic agenda and my desire to represent the project's participants. So far, asking those participants to produce their own written representations of their experiences has seemed impracticable for many reasons. Because I still plan one chapter representing those participants, my ethnography's structure embodies this tension rather than resolving it. This structure—and its shaping of my ethnography's content—is one way to deal with the problem of representing others. Of course, it is not workable for all ethnographic projects or subjects. But perhaps it affords a way to rethink ethnographic representations by pushing us as ethnographers to imagine how we might restructure our inquiries so that they entail group writing projects of autoethnography that implicate the ethnographer as one of the ethnographic subjects, as a participant in the processes represented.

The tensions of representation still remain. As the person structuring the ethnographic text and writing historical chapters that contextualize the community center project, I am positioning not only my own representation of our project but also my colleagues' representations as well. I am still struggling, then, to design an ethnographic structure that entails a truly *joint* endeavor of inquiry and representation. Enabling such a project would require a rethinking of "authorship," of what an academic project is. It would also involve structural problems: community activists' time and other resources are already thinly spread. Undertaking an ethnography that is fully autoethnographic, fully mutual in its conception and execution, would mean struggling with the questions of what would be the stakes, or benefits, for nonacademic writers in producing such a project. Similarly, it would mean struggling with the problem of professional credentialing, of ethnographers' need to produce texts and accrue publications that enable them to complete their degrees, to secure jobs, to get tenure, promotion, and so on. These practical questions all constitute substantive theoretical issues that we, as ethnographers—and as teachers and academics struggling to build coalitions with those whom we represent—must address.

Although my ethnographic study will undoubtedly work within, rather than resolve, these tensions, I hope that continually struggling to revise my theoretical frame for doing ethnography will push the practice closer to an ethics it can never fully enact. Despite its inevitable shortfalls, for me, this kind of ethnography is still worth undertaking. It is one of the few ways to bring academic discourses into direct negotiation with the discourses of those represented by academic texts. Even more importantly, as an effort to design a collaborative form, a collective community-academy project, it offers a means to build partnerships for transformation, a means that is noticeably absent from much of both contemporary critical theory and composition studies.

Notes

1. "Forties" is slang for forty-ounce bottles of beer, and the word "blunt" denotes marijuana cigarettes.

2. *Debating Muslims: Cultural Dialogues in Postmodernity and Tradition*, by Michael M. J. Fischer and Mehdi Abedi, is an ethnography that impressively embodies this kind of combination and does so, as its title suggests, to foster negotiation among competing conceptual frameworks.

7

Writing Through the Grapevine
The Influence of Social Network Clusters on Team-Written Texts

Geoffrey A. Cross

In investigating the creation of collaboratively written texts in the workplace, we have chiefly focused upon the visible members of the writing group—that is, the individuals who meet to inscribe the document. Each individual, however, may be closely affiliated with informal groups in the organization, small clusters or "micro-networks" of people who construct "webs of meaning," in this case versions of classroom or organizational reality. Clifford Geertz (1973), drawing on the work of sociologist Max Weber, has stated that human beings are animals suspended in webs of meaning that they themselves have spun (5). Although social construction of meaning cannot account for all that we know—we can receive experiential knowledge in our encounters with nature, for example, knowledge that cold makes us shiver, and we may also receive knowledge or guidance from intuition or revelation—nevertheless, socially acquired knowledge is a major portion of what and how we know.

To (literally) extend the metaphor of webs of meaning, we can think about them as resilient spiders' webs. When we choose to collaborate on documents, we do so at least in part to create a larger web: to incorporate more knowledge than one person has about a problem. But often this goal is not realized. Professionals responding to Ede and Lunsford's (1990) extensive survey of group writing in several different fields reported that forty-two percent of their group writing experiences were "less than productive" (45–50). Moreover, our research on

The author wishes to thank Barbara Blackburn and Paul Tuttle for responding to a draft of this article.

classroom collaboration indicates that writing groups are not always successful (e.g., Burnett, 1991; Fleming et al., in press; Kelvin and Leonard, in press).

Perhaps one reason for less-than-productive collaborations is that typically the knowledge intended to be combined is socially constructed and politically situated. Maher and Tretault (1994) further explain the nature of socially constructed knowledge: "the knower's specific position . . . is always defined by gender, race, class, and other socially significant dimensions" (22). Informal networks often contribute to each collaborator's identity informed by race, class, gender, and political situation. The opposing and/or similar positions of collaborators' respective webs of meaning can cause problems in collaborative groups.

For example, suppose that liberal and conservative groups are working together in Congress to draft a plan to balance the federal budget. Half the writing team members are, in life outside the collaborative writing group, attached to a communication network/web of meaning anchored in a remote location opposing the anchoring site of the others' web. The powerfully elastic webs pull writing group members apart from each other and back to their opposing anchorages. Group members' relatively feeble efforts to connect these webs, interweaving the far-stretched strands in a team-written document, may be futile. On the other hand, the webs may overlap nearly completely if all group members are in the same informal communication network. This overlap often makes collaboration easy but unproductive because no new area is covered. To avoid either a collaboration that covers no new ground or irreconcilable differences among group members, we need to focus on the informal networks that may often inform members of writing groups and form or deform their written products.

Composition's "social turn" has led us to investigate not only the academic but also the nonacademic settings into which we send nearly all of our students to do most of the life writing they will ever do. A few composition studies of either academic or nonacademic settings have mentioned informal social networks in passing. For example, Brandt (1986) calls for research on "the resources available to language users in the social and linguistic networks they participate in" (144). Selzer (1993) notes that electronic mail networks may contribute to the intertextuality of a document. He also mentions informal networks of colleagues and advisors as one aspect of the broader, intertextual Barthesian "network" of meaning, "the sum total of all the voices drawn by a writer into his or her developing text and . . . all the voices heard by readers in the experience of that writing" (176). This is an important distinction because the notion of extant social networks can be conflated with the broader intertextual definition of networks.

Three other studies consider social networks in more depth. In a study that considers how social networks relate to computer manual use, Mirel (1991) found that because their tacit needs conflicted with the organizations' goals, university cashiers did not use a new computer manual that had been thoroughly tested for comprehensibility. Cashiers' progress in learning the computer systems was slowed because of their preference for informal user networks that not only provided information (however limited) but also provided for affective needs ("fellowship").

The influence of informal networks on students in first-year composition was investigated by Brooke (1987) and Vander Lei (1995). Although this research does not employ many techniques of network analysis developed by communication studies, the important findings show the rich potential of this method. Brooke's well-known study shows that informal student networks in class supported students' resistance to the roles provided by the "official" culture. As Brooke notes, drawing on the work of sociologist Erving Goffman, students often define themselves by distancing themselves from groups to which they belong. Of course, even if networks are what individuals react against, they need to be uncovered to understand the motives of collaborators.

How social networks extend beyond the walls of the classroom is the focus of Vander Lei's study, which found that although the seven students observed networked with classmates for information on assignments and to get their papers to class in their absence, they most often chose nonclassmates to read their papers and help with audience analysis. Which function networking served made a great difference in their success on their ostensibly nongroup assignments. Networking could be a distraction from acquiring college writing skills: Mitch networked about his papers with unhelpful family members and spent much time that could have been devoted to composition in maintaining his presence in his family and working at a part-time job. Networking could be a dependency: Angie enrolled in the class at Arizona State with three other students from her Chicago suburb and while writing papers was constantly on the phone with classmate Janie, one of the Chicago group, asking how sentences sounded. She was also in daily contact with her writer mother. While Angie seemed to crave social interaction, Janie felt imposed on and said that her network sometimes blocked her own composing. Neither Angie nor Janie had a very strong task representation of the somewhat vague assignment, and the blind-leading-the-blind situation was not a huge success. A network did contribute greatly to the most successful writer of the study, Ian, who got advice from his girlfriend, a strong writer who was a year ahead in school, and from his literate, incisive father.[1]

Pursuit of a more thorough understanding of the context of writing has led researchers to call for network analysis and has led to some rich initial findings: Mirel presents an excellent example of the power of informal networks upon ostensible readers/computer users, and Brooke and Vander Lei vividly depict and analyze individual student writers networking with informal groups. Nevertheless, no one has applied the formal study of communication networks to collaborative writing to focus on the possible roles and influences of the grapevine on formal collaborative groups.

Functions of Networks

As communication research tells us, although formal communication routes, often following the organizational chart, are established and controlled by officially appointed leaders, the informal system is based on social relations (Davis, 1977). Informal groups and dyads (pairs) often form because individuals are not sure their views about the organization are useful, so they look to others to confirm or increase their confidence in their perceptions (Erickson 1988, 101). In informal pairs or groups, people can get advice without having to call official attention to their seeking help (Blau, 1974, 7). Besides fulfilling the individual's need to clarify his or her perceptions, informal groups and dyads form for the exchange of goods and services, to meet affective needs, and to influence others (Tichy, Tushman, and Fombrun, 1979). In Vander Lei's study we see that two of these functions combined. Two charismatic male students who missed classes had other, less-popular students serve as "go-fers," who brought them notes and assignments. In exchange for their service, the go-fers received an affective payoff of recognition from the popular students. Individuals can form networks to discuss production (routine work) or innovation (Farace, Monge, and Russell 1977). Vander Lei's study illustrates this point in that most classmates discussed routine work whereas writers relied on out-of-class networks for getting innovative feedback on papers. These groups or dyads often construct a common perception of organizational or classroom reality. However, some informal groups and dyads are not linked to each other in any significant way (Fig. 1) and often do not share a common perception of organizational reality. As Smircich notes, reality is not merely passively understood but instead enacted by individuals, and in organizations in which there exist "multiple meaning systems or 'counterrealities' that may be in competition with each other" (1983, 162). The "official reality" of the corporation is often presented in corporate documents such as policy statements, plans, and annual reports. In a group writing process, representatives of different organizational realities may compete for the prize of making their reality the "official view" of the corporation. By defining the company in the area addressed by the document, the prevailing group can display its power in the organization.

Structures and Analysis of Networks

By using the theory and findings of network research, we can more fully articulate the multiple realities of the social context of writing. Network analysis depicts social structures as a series of nodes (social system members) and sets of ties showing their interconnections. Network analysts have identified four entities operating in or outside informal networks: 1) groups or clusters, including coalitions and cliques. *Coalitions* are short-lived groups that typically form to achieve limited political objectives. *Cliques* are long-term groups that pursue a variety of purposes. Members interact more with

Figure 1

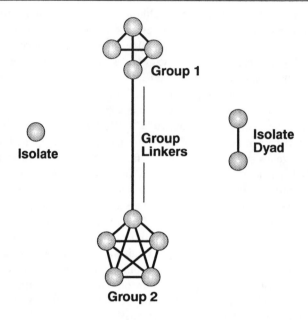

each other than they do with other people in the population studied. 2) Group linkers are members who unite two or more groups. 3) *Dyads* are pairs who interact more with each other than with the rest of the population examined. 4) *Isolates* are individuals who have nearly no informal communication with the population studied. Groups and dyads can differ from other groups and dyads in their strength or intensity—the number of data, goods, or services influence or affect those flows (Monge and Eisenberg, 315). One property of the ties is symmetry—whether people enter into the same kind of relationship with each other. The go-fers and the popular students, for example, did not have symmetrical relationships. Another property of linkages is reciprocity, the extent to which the two individuals presumed to be linked report the same relationship.

Network structures can be viewed not only from this "micro" level but also from the "macro level, looking at the entire network (Wasserman & Faust, 1994, xiii). Complex studies view the dyad, triad, or small group in relation to the entire network, tying together, as Wasserman and Faust (1994) note, "interdependent parts that constitute micro- and macro-social orders" (xiii).

What research methods are used to investigate networks? Communications network research to date has been nearly exclusively quantitative. Data has been gathered in many ways, including asking subjects to log their communications; observing the subjects communicate; asking in question-naires about subjects' overall patterns of interaction; following a message intended for a specific receiver and recording the path the message takes to get there; and studying the diffusion of any message throughout the organization (Farace, Monge, and Russell, 1977, 208–209). Wasserman and Faust (1994) provide a vast repertoire of statistical techniques with which to analyze these and other kinds of network data. In addition, computer programs (e.g., UCINET and KRACKPLOT) can help identify and plot networks (Borgatti et al., 1992; Krackhardt, Blythe, and McGrath, 1995). These quantitative approaches have greatly advanced the understanding of network structures; however, these techniques do not show what is being communicated, so network researchers are calling for qualitative studies (Monge and Eisenberg, 1987; Fulk and Steinfield, 1990). Beyond that, a multimodal approach employing both quantitative and qualitative ethnographic methods could be very effective in tracing the effect of the grapevine upon classroom and organizational processes such as group writing.

The potential of such an approach for both ethnographies of classroom and nonacademic writing is suggested by Morrill's (1991) multimodal study. Morrill conducted a 453-hour observation of participants investigating whether top-level executives in "loose-knit" and "densely-knit" organizations handled conflicts differently. Not only how executives networked but moreover what generally was discussed was investigated. Morrill determined whether the social network of the company was "loosely knit" or "densely knit" by performing several procedures. He began by conducting an ethnographic interview with each executive, after which he asked the following sociometric questions: 1) Who among the executives do you talk to at least two-to-three times a week about work-related issues only? 2) Who among the executives do you receive information from two-to-three times a week to make timely and effective decisions? 3) Which executives, if any, have you called on in the last six months to be an ally during conflicts with other executives? 4) In whom, if anyone, do you confide about interpersonal or work-related problems you or a colleague are experiencing on the job?

From his data, Morrill next constructed "people-by-people" matrices—for the "loose-knit" accounting firm, for example, a nineteen-by-nineteen executive matrix. These matrices plotted the existence of social ties between executives at the company. Morrill also conducted statistical analyses of density, the extent to which links that might exist among people do exist. He not only calculated the density of all social contacts, but he also computed the density of different kinds of ties—whether an executive just spoke to another executive or whether he or she also gossiped together and/or were allies. In so doing, Morrill made it possible to trace several networks relating to the above questions: Question 1—networks of executives in frequent communication, Question 2—networks of executives between whom important information is frequently communicated (subset of previous network), Question 3—allies (possible subset of network one or one *and* two), and Question 4—networks of "gossip" (possible subset of one or one and two and/or three).

To compare the amounts of intracompany executive networking at the two different companies, Morrill compared mean densities of both uniplex (one kind of link) executive networks and multiplex (two or more kinds of links, e.g., executives share information and are allies) executive networks. Results showed that the accounting company had relatively low-density means, indicating a loose-knit executive network, whereas at the other company, a toy manufacturer, the executive network was densely knitted. Morrill then drew upon data from observations and interviews of nearly all executives to show that conflicts over serious and non-serious issues were handled very differently in the tightly versus loosely networked companies. Executives at the loosely-knit accounting firm tended to use nonconfrontational techniques, particularly temporary avoidance and tolerance, to address either minor or serious conflicts. By contrast, executives at the manufacturer tended to confront each other during both minor and serious conflicts. Nearly one-third of manufacturing executives' expressions about conflict mentioned engaging in ritualized, high-stakes verbal "duels" at highly visible meetings.

Morrill additionally drew on ethnographic data to render a typical day at the office for an executive at each company. Such ethnographic portraits of subjects are often used as epitomes of larger social phenomena. One value of using network analysis before creating these ethnographic portraits is that one can choose an epitome from a map of the social groups. One should not select an epitome if one does not understand the larger social phenomenon the epitome supposedly represents. Of course, a network map is not the territory. Qualitative research can help determine the strength of influence of the various dyads or groups mapped. Studies have shown that social influence does not require face-to-face interaction or even conscious attempts to change actors' behaviors (Marsden and Friedkin, 1994, 4). Some groups may be highly influential but not directly linked to other groups. Qualitative methods added to statistical network analysis help ensure that the map does not mislead us about the territory and that the epitomes are representative of the cultures.

When should one apply network analysis during ethnographic research of collaborative writing? The site is like a HyperCard stack. When the ethnographer enters it, she or he is at the first screen. This screen is full of unfamiliar information, in which, everything looks important. Indeed, one could spend all the time in the field simply covering events on the surface, but the danger is "thin description," presenting a host of insignificant minutiae. "Front-ending" the study, of course, having a definite conceptual framework and a specific set of research questions or hypotheses, can provide focus (Miles and Huberman, 1994). Many layers beneath the surface may need excavation to come closest to apprehending the social context, however, a context not apparent when the conceptual frame and research questions were devised. Certainly, we can revise our conceptual frame and questions as we go along to accommodate what we learn of the context. Yet while the "submerged" connotations may surface in a collaborative meeting where different members advocate their different networks' world views and interests, the subcultural origins of these concepts may never be apparent to the ethnographer who has not conducted network analysis. For example, in the classrooms, "slacker" group members who seem to be individualistically opposing the official "good student" role in a collaboration may actually be trying to maintain the morés of a group with which they are affiliated on campus. Thus, applying network analysis methods early in the field—not only gathering data but also plotting the network—is optimal, as Miles and Huberman note (1994, 104).

Yet although plotting networks early in the field experience seems optimal, is it possible? During the early part of fieldwork, building rapport with subjects is especially important, particularly so until they become reasonably comfortable about providing information. Ethnographers often do not begin audiotaping until after some purely observational sessions have been completed. Under such circumstances, how does one get information about who talks to whom about what, when "behind the scenes," even when in the "smoke-filled rooms?" Fortunately, the sociometric questions asked in network analysis are often innocuous, for example, asking an executive to log who she or he talked to every day. It may be also that only the most innocuous questions are asked or are asked early in the study. Furthermore, network analysis should not be used in some studies in which access to informants is particularly tentative. In some other cases, more sensitive questions should be asked in the middle or toward the end of the study as the context dictates. Even conducting end-of-fieldwork questioning that forces one to plot the network after leaving the field could be of great analytic value and could inspire a few follow-up questions over the phone or in interviews that might make all the difference in understanding the site.

Although this practice may yield rich information about the social context, is it ethical for the researcher to withhold his or her intention from the observed? Because researchers cannot assume they understand what is important in the lives of participants, or even which questions are pertinent, some feminist ethnographers (e.g., Kirsch and Ritchie, 1995, 13–15) assert that participants should be fully briefed on all research objectives before any interviews start and the participants should be continuously updated on the ethnographer's evolving view of the site. The danger of this approach to "naturalistic" research of writing processes is to make those observed unnaturally self-conscious of their actions and to cause them, intentionally or unintentionally, to change their normal behavior. Certainly, the ethnographer's presence at the beginning of the study makes most informants self-conscious, but the duration of fieldwork soon makes the ethnographer a very familiar part of the landscape. Telling the observed about perceived emerging "patterns" of activity, however, may not only make them more self-conscious but also make them intentionally reenact the patterns to appear consistent, making the researcher's conjecture a self-fulfilling prophecy. Another danger in a networking study is for the observed to react abnormally against group morés in order not to appear to the ethnographer to be a "follower." The observed may also become unusually obedient to a subcultural code to display solidarity with a high-status network. In any of these cases, the final conclusions and recommendations that the ethnographer makes to improve the writing processes of the observed may have no bearing on the observed's standard processes of writing. Still, this is not to say that ethnographers should misrepresent those observed. In indirect ways, researchers should look for disconfirming evidence to any of their evolving understandings. Moreover, the observed can respond to drafts of the ethnographer's end research report. This response should be incorporated into the ethnographer's final research report either in the body of the text or in an appendix.

What strategic research questions should researchers using network analysis ask? Looking at the networking diagram (see Fig. 1), if the isolate, the isolated dyad, and one member from each group collaborate, we could for starters see how their networks (or lack of them for the isolate) affect their performance in the writing group from the standpoint of:

Power: Who is well connected to the most powerful members of the organization or classroom (e.g., the instructor or a student leader)? Does the writing group give her or his ideas more weight than it gives to the isolate's?

Generative ability: Does a widely networked person have more or fewer ideas than an isolate or dyad?

Style: It has been asserted that voice is "always about class and race and gender" (Maher and Tretault, 96). Network analysis combined with qualitative research can get at some immediate social manifestations of race, class, and gender in a person's life. The method can investigate whether each network has a trademark style or whether an isolate is less likely to give up stylistic ownership of a text.

Interorganizational influence: Do outsiders have significant influence on collaboration via networks? Parents like Angie's mother may have a strong although indirect effect on collaborative groups, for example.

Gender: Feminine ways of learning have been described as connected and relational, and masculine approaches have been characterized as separate and rational. Critics have, however, attacked these dichotomies as false. Network analysis along with qualitative research could add a new dimension to the empirical study of gender differences in collaboration by showing the extent to which collaborators' knowledge came from connecting with networks outside the composition class.

Technology: Telephones, fax machines, and the Internet all can extend participant networks far beyond the walls of any academic or nonacademic institution. What virtual social networks do collaborative group members belong to? Do these networks differ from face-to-face networks in their amount of influence or other properties? Not only who is linked to whom but also who communicates openly and who merely lurks (i.e., reads others' posts) are critical questions in this age of the smart machine (Zuboff, 1988). Rice's (1994) bibliographic essay on network theory and computer-mediated communication systems is an excellent beginning for composition researchers interested in using network analysis on a local or on the global "net."

We need to look not only at how networks affect collaboration but also at how collaboration affects networks. Organizations have been defined as streams of evolving relationships. Classes can be seen the same way. As Vander Lei notes, "while writing essays for school, students compose not only discourses but also self-concepts and relationships with family, friends, instructors, and classmates" (169). How does collaboration change these relationships and modify networks? Further, does the overall classroom or organizational climate determine the influence of members' nonwriting-group networks? If there is a supportive climate—nonjudgmental, consensual, honest, empathetic, open to innovation—is the writing group members' reliance on outside "support networks" less? Alternatively, no matter what the organizational climate, if the *writing group* has a supportive climate, is the members' reliance upon outside "support networks" less?

Ethnography must locate not only the position of the observed but also the position of the observer. For purposes of self-reflexivity, the ethnographer could trace his or her own social networks during research to denote both the context and the process of interpretation.

Beyond data-gathering questions, network analysis also raises questions for researchers about the best mode or modes of representation. Of course, the traditional hard copy research article with network diagrams remains useful. Nevertheless, the construction and influence of the webs of knowledge may be best rendered today by supplementing or replacing the standard research article with a hypertext version. Such an "article" might at the surface be the finished written product of the collaboration. Important ideas and phrasings in this final document would be demarked by icons and "hot buttoned" (linked) to other screens that describe in words or record on film and/or audiotape the informal groups that contributed this idea or otherwise influenced its being put in the final product. Network analysis using hypertext could show how some webs of meaning are woven together into a collaborative text and perhaps how other webs are excluded from the final product. The hypertext flowchart that plots the hypertext lexia (screens) and links would give an overview of the interrelation of these networks. On the other hand, "drilling down" through a HyperCard stack to trace any local, subcultural origins of the text would allow the reader to experience more fully the dialogical properties of language. This experience more completely represents human relationships perhaps too busily and two-dimensionally sketched by network diagrams alone. It enhances the rendering of a culture, by distinguishing the textual equivalents of blinks from winks and faked winks (that is, the connotations of the signs in the written product) and the webs of meaning/social realities and their constructors.

Besides these research considerations, network analysis has implications for practitioners and facilitators of collaboration. Vander Lei's study strongly suggests that high-quality networking can contribute to high-quality writing. Encouraging students to examine their own networks and if necessary to network with more experienced, successful writers could improve their abilities as individual and group writers. Networking could be encouraged in dormitories by starting writing support groups there, perhaps facilitated by writing laboratory or writing-across-the-curriculum personnel.

In nonacademic organizations, because formal channels are not always effective means of gathering information, a major factor in the selection of group members should be the number of informal networks they are in and their number of contacts within these networks. Properly constructed writing teams tapping key networks can favorably influence whether the text is read by the intended audience, and whether the text achieves its purpose with that audience. Incorporating the perspectives of many networks into organizational policies and manuals would be particularly valuable because the better the coverage, the better the fit between "the book"—written policy—and the culture.

Network analysis will help the ethnographer of the classroom deal with the quandary of how to study this temporary community, this evanescent culture. Network analysis can also be a way for teachers and collaborators to make the hidden social webs of meaning visible so gaps can be spanned. Considered in the light of network analysis coupled with ethnographic research methods, collaborative writing group members may be composite characters, the nexi of networks. We need to conduct ethnographic research in both qualitative and quantitative modes to investigate to what extent the *groups* behind the group determine the outcome of collaboratively written texts.

Notes

1. Certainly, the ethnographer has no right to independently assess the ultimate value of any of the social networks in which the observed participate. Nevertheless, since a primary goal of composition research is to produce knowledge that contributes to writing improvement, the ethnographer can assess which kinds of networks and network dynamics promote the advancement of students' academic and professional writing skills. Teachers can encourage students to seek a network of writers—not necessarily to the exclusion of other networks—that can help the students acquire writing skills that will help him or her avoid marginalization by society.

8

Writing Bio(Life) into Ethnography

Ruoyi Wu

Two Western genres, autobiography and ethnography, share some similarities to me as a Chinese whose culture is, as I read somewhere, "notorious" for being synthetical. Supposedly, the former is about the self and the latter about the other, but both are rooted in the subject/object dichotomy. Historically, the two genres appeared and developed simultaneously in the modern period when Western interest in the self led to studies of others as its mirror.[1] Recently, the concepts of *auto* (self) and *ethno* (other people) have been challenged by postmodern theorists as nothing but textual constructs.[2] No individual, they assume, can study either herself or another culture objectively. More importantly, women and other minorities strengthen the challenges by frequently blurring the line between the self and other when writing in both genres. As a consequence of such challenges, anthropologists and autobiography critics have shifted their focuses from the self and other to *graphy* (writing), for texts are accessible when reality is not.[3]

Ethno-bio-graphy

Bio (life), the one element that the two genres do not share, needs more attention among composition researchers. This is because stressing either *ethno* or *graphy* cannot deal with the complexity of multicultural lives ethnographers encounter in their research. I am arguing that we should write *life* into ethnography to produce what I call *ethnobiography*, writing that includes the historical contexts of both the researcher and the researched. In other words, we should present our differences in our projects rather than focusing on textuality only. As feminist critics Bella Brodzki and Celeste Schenck (1988) assert

77

> . . . the duplicitous and complicitous relationship of "life" and "art" in autobiographical modes is precisely the point. To elide it in the name of eliminating the "facile assumption of referentiality" is dangerously to ignore the crucial referentiality of class, race, and sexual orientation; it is to beg serious political questions. (12–13)

Translated into ethnographic research, the interdependence of life and writing is "precisely the point." We need to discuss what is written and what is not by comparing our researchers' experiences with generic expectations implicit in ethnography.

This emphasis on the tension between life and texts also aims to deconstruct the subject/object polarity as well as solve the paranoia in representing the self and others that postmodern theory of subjectivity has left in the humanities and social sciences.[4] It will, accordingly, overcome "one-sided knowledge control and discourse dominance" between the researcher and the researched resulting from ethnography's original role in colonial history and its concept of "Other" (Khare, 1992, 2). By focusing on specifics, *ethnobiography* also aims to dissolve other artificial categories such as reason and emotion, the insider and outsider, and the observer and participant.

Therefore, ethnobiography is not just "narrative," or "confessional," or "dialogic" ethnography.[5] Unlike such alternatives that may still skirt around experiences, it will specify all *bios* with their multicultural values rather than analyzing textual elements. Ethnobiographic texts will allow us to avoid what Kirsch and Richie (1995) call "superficial reflexivity," such as the statement so commonly attached to the beginning of articles: "I am a white, middle-class woman from a midwestern university doing research" (9). At the same time, ethnobiography will not go "beyond the personal," as Kirsch and Richie propose. The phrase—a typical way of theorizing in composition—unproductively dichotomizes the personal and the social. Yet in crosscultural encounters, the personal is intertwined with the material and the political. Thus, by *life* I mean not only researchers' interactions with informants, but the usually unwritten parts of our ethnographic texts, all pretexts and contexts and subtexts. In life, to transcend the personal is simply impossible.

Ethno *Bios* in My Research

These theoretical reflections all came out of my own ethnographic study of one ESL writing class and particularly my dilemma as a bicultural researcher who felt uncomfortable with the role of participant observer. For my research, I wanted to study ESL students' self-presentations in autobiographical writing as reflected in a first-year writing class. I observed one ESL class and conducted some case studies.[6] While I was studying self-culture relations in autobiography and doing ethnography, I began to wonder how an ethnographer could avoid being personal and how an autobiographer could focus completely on herself. I also began to question the technique of participant observation.

Both limiting and limited, it implied the kinds of stories to be told: one kind of writing (scientific), one kind of researcher (objective), and one kind of observer-observed relationship (hierarchical).

My discomfort with the technique resulted from some conflicts between my sense of self and my required role as a researcher. First, my often fluid position in relation to the "native" and research community made me ambivalent about my identity as a researcher. Moreover, as a Chinese who was brought up during the Cultural Revolution, I had a sense of self totally different from the one prescribed by the dual role: it was a self inseparable from society, although this cultural ideal was geographically and historically limited. Knowing that my research was underwritten by my bicultural values, I realized that when portraying specifics of their multicultural experiences, researchers necessarily crossed slippery boundaries between the self and other, between the insider and outsider, and between various genres.

Before I began my study, I learned that a key issue in ethnographic research was the researcher's relationship with the culture she studied. The ideal balanced role for researchers is participant observation, best explained by Clifford Geertz in his famous article "Native's Point of View" (1983). Geertz borrows two related concepts, "experience-near" and "experience-distant," from the psychoanalyst Heinz Kohut to show that we can know natives even though we are not part of their group. The crucial question to Geertz is how one should

> deploy them so as to produce an interpretation of the way a people lives which is neither imprisoned within their mental horizons, an ethnography of witchcraft as written by a witch, nor systematically deaf to the distinctive tonalities of their existence, an ethnography of witchcraft as written by a geometer. (57).

This balance between the two perspectives—being a witch and a geometer while writing about witchcraft—had been my ideal in approaching research, along with the standard that a good study is "theoretically driven."

Once I started my actual research though, I recognized many possible shades of differences and unclear areas between the two extremes. No clearly defined role was available for me standing between cultures. Being neither a real witch nor a geometer, I was supposed to do two opposite things: to get involved while remaining detached. Detachment was further reinforced by the required "theoretical drivenness," resulting in more ambivalence to me, because analytical categories had to be based on the research community's epistemology. Although I constantly struggled with the various theories that might "contain" writers like myself, I still cherished neutral methodology as key to our understanding of ESL writers. That is, I spent a lot of time searching for a smaller "mismatch" between theory and my data.

The major questions I asked before going to the field were framed not only by my readings in Western rhetoric but also by my Chinese values. I wanted to study ESL writers' self-presentation. For one thing, the heated debate between social and expressive rhetorics and their tendency to oppose the self and society as well as personal and academic discourse did not seem relevant to me. As a Chinese, I had never felt one was more significant than the other; they became one in writing. Moreover, the ESL research community was limited by its dominant linguistic paradigm, so there were few cross-cultural studies done in either the self or autobiography. Even the major pedagogical goals for them were correctness rather than self-expression.[7] In short, ESL writers were excluded from other groups due to their cultural and linguistic differences.

As an ESL writer myself, I did not see any sense in such gaps between mainstream and ESL writing. Accordingly, I wanted to explore various connections between the self and culture among ESL writers in a classroom. I used what I called the "cultural self" as an explanatory construct, but I found later that I had actually poked at "a wasps' nest" (a Chinese expression): the entire Western culture seemed to depend on this subject/object polarity. I could define cultural self only in negative terms: it was not Descartes' metaphysical entity, nor Peter Elbow's inner voice, nor even Goffman's identity in role negotiation, for all these accounts derive, directly or indirectly, from the Western notion of the self as an individual apart from society. What I did not question, though, was my sheer confidence in myself as a researcher who was able to investigate other selves with her deep-rooted culture-specific values.

When I observed the ESL class focused on autobiographical writing, I felt uneasy about my dual role as observer and participant. On the first day, I asked the instructor if she could introduce me to the class because I could not do it, being there neither as the teacher nor as a student. Within one week, a Korean student asked me whether she could borrow my notes, for she could not always understand what was going on. I felt I was a little selfish when I told her that I could not help her because this was "my" research, not class notes. When it was time to ask the class to sign the "Informed Consent"—legal forms required by my university's Human Subjects Committee, I was paralyzed.[8] With its suspicious legal language, the form itself might alienate those I was studying and break any trust they had in me. I was assured, however, that the form was the only way to protect them, and accordingly, me from any legal suit. Yet far from being convinced, I again asked the instructor to explain to the class why they had to sign the form. As a result, one of the most interesting subjects refused to sign, saying (what I would have done in his place) that I could use his writing, but he did not want to sign the form.

All these examples, I realized later, required me to draw a clearer line between myself and others than I liked. I did not want to stress my researcher identity so as to interrupt the flow of the class, nor to be so selfish as to keep my notes to myself, nor treat others in contractual terms that might imply a lack of interpersonal responsibility and trust. To me personally, forms were threatening, because during the Cultural Revolution I had had to fill out many that would stamp me as a member of certain "marked" groups. I was sure that some students might have similar feelings.

This ambivalence lasted throughout the whole process of research. What I wanted most was an unobtrusiveness achieved through both my effort not to interfere with the class and my desire to feel as part of them. In other words, though I consciously intended to "go native," I could not participate and observe at the same time. I had conflicting fears. First, I was afraid that if I participated actively, the students might not benefit because the class would be spent on my interests. Second, I might also lead some in the class to say things similar to my assumptions so that the intricacies of the group would be lost. Third, if I told them what to do, they might end up with a grade they did not like (they saw me partially as a teacher). Fourth, if I did not play an active role, I might also run the risk of not getting various subtle cultural differences I intended to seek. Thus, I followed my instinct in being a "quieter" presence to be accepted.

Conflicting Views of Self-Other Relations

To find out why I had felt uncomfortable with the role, I read some literature about researchers' roles, "reflexivity," and "confessional tales,"[9] yet all seemed to be based on the model of the researcher as an individual who could separate herself from the culture she observed and who was different from the latter too. Some theorists used Augustine, Rousseau, and Montaigne—all "classical" autobiographers and individualists—to show thinking as a self-reflexive activity. To Rousseau, this reflexive ability is defined as "regard[ing] oneself as an other and to be aware of oneself as his instrument of observation" (Babcock, 1980, 3). To distinguish the four extremes of data, subjects, the research community, and the researcher in my study was hard for me: my bicultural background located me in an unclear locus with regard to all of them.[10]

I understood then ethnography was a genre used by Western researchers to study far away, exotic cultures. The ideal fieldworker was someone who could distance herself from others while actively participating in their lives. But when the researcher studied a group mentally close to her, the line between us and them became smudged. That is why I sensed a mismatch between how I felt and what was required of me in research. Besides, I could not visualize myself playing multiple roles like putting on different garments as Goffman describes everybody doing. My obligation to the research participants as well as to the instructor raised a major ethical question. It was not probing into others' "private" lives—for anything presented in writing was socially significant to me—but trying not to be "selfish" when working with the people who were helping me. Such a double consciousness led me to question my own assumptions about culture and self, including my findings and interpretations of the students' self-presentations.

At root was a conflict regarding the self-other relation, between that inscribed in ethnography and that inscribed in the Chinese ideal self. My upbringing on one hand did not allow me to see myself as apart from people like me (there were quite a few Chinese and Asian students in the class), a sense of self far from the one implicated in the dual role. As LuMing Mao (1994) points out, among the Chinese, the individual has "a symbiotic relationship" (16) with her community, one that is untranslatable into English. For us, as Lawrence D. Kincaid writes, the part and whole "ultimately cannot be separated . . . there is no part *and* whole but rather one part/whole. Each 'one' defines the other, and indeed *is* the other" (9). As the individual is not opposed to the community, "to subdue oneself" becomes part of the self-realizing process (20).

This social ideal of self is ethical, aesthetic, and philosophical. Its counterpart of importance in Western culture would be the post-Romantic individualistic self so prevalent in all areas of life.[11] Neither concept is realistic, but each has rhetorical power over members of a culture. When I was growing up, this social ideal was smoothly blended into the teachings of the Communist Party. In addition, the holistic Chinese identity was reinforced by our nondistinction between the two sexes or races as well as our long-time resistance to outside influences. Living in the United States, I have become more "gendered" and more "colored." In this multicultural society oriented toward analytical thinking, members have to be categorized to have a social identity. Yet my Chinese self was so real to me that when the instructor assigned one chapter on gender identity, I was worried that it would distract the students from their emphasis on the cultural dimension of their selves. Now I am glad that this part of their autobiographies has provided me with more complex dimensions of the ESL students' identities and material for a cross-cultural analysis of gender. For better or worse, my Chinese heritage has become so much of me that I have to remind myself all the time how bicultural my thinking is. To admit that I am equally influenced by American and Chinese rhetorics simply does not sound "good" to my generation with our Cultural Revolution mentality.

Limitations of Participant Observation

On the other hand, the ethnographer's dual role is not as obviously question-able as many methods in more hard-nosed social sciences. In fact, it is often seen as a method that assures reflexivity.[12] To play the two roles simul-taneously, however, is "a task at least as delicate, if a bit less magical, as putting oneself into someone else's skin" (Geertz, 1983, 58). Everywhere we see examples of great disparities between the natives and observers. In his ethnography textbook, for instance, David M. Fetterman (1989) draws a clear line between *them* as objects of study and *us* as researchers. In a typical description of a fire threatening the natives, Fetterman calmly considers the pros and cons of the situation from the researcher's perspective (94). Other than being bound by the obligation as a participant, the researcher is depicted as detached from the natives' tragedy. If this imagined researcher is watching a fire among her own people, does she ever have time to consider all the factors before she acts? Does she remain insensitive to the group under study?

Anthropologist Barbara Tedlock (1991) sharply points out that what lies behind the ideal role are assumed polarities "between objectivity and subjectivity, between scientist and native, and between Self and Other," (71) with an implication that only an outsider can be objective. Insiders, treated as the other by the researcher, are ranked lower in this hierarchical relation, so they naturally become more "vulnerable to value conflicts because they are unable to maintain a safe emotional distance from the communities they research" (Moss, 1992, 163). That is, the farther away you are emotionally from what you study, the better off your research is in avoiding "bad" science, though the insider perspective is essential in cross-cultural understanding.

I would think that neither an insider, nor an outsider, nor a bicultural observer can separate her feelings from her thoughts. All of these categories, the subjective and objective, the emotional and rational, the personal and social, and the insider and outsider, are social constructs that Westerners use to make sense out of complicated human life. In my case, how could I write about witchcraft without revealing my inclination as a witch? How could I stick to an outsider's unbiased lens while my own location in the world was not only clear but even at stake?

Even ethnographers with a clearer outsider view cannot avoid such vulnerability. They cannot get rid of their cultural baggage of values or separate themselves from others completely. We know some anthropologists from the West who "went native" and never came back to their own society (Tedlock, 70). I wonder if their imaginative universe converged with the others,' or if the two were so divergent that they had to give up their outsider status to "go native." Maybe their rich imagination and the dire reality they faced caused them to become bicultural or at least grow closer to natives while playing dual roles. The other extreme was the well-known anthropologist Bronislaw Malinowski who shocked his field by writing an unprofessional diary: he used rude language to describe the natives. According to Geertz (1983), Malinowski's was an epistemological issue more than a moral one, since his "voice from the grave merely dramatizes it as a human dilemma over and above a professional one" (56). In composition studies, such cases are rare due to the less exotic cultures we study. Yet these between-culture lives do reveal that it is hard to distinguish the two roles or to separate the emotional from the rational.

No wonder the 1970s witnessed a shift in anthropology from participant observation to an emphasis on "coparticipation," as Tedlock tells us. Instead of trying to get involved and be detached at the same time, ethnographers attempt to describe the cultural "encounter" between the natives and themselves.

(Tedlock, 69). Now "both the Self and Other are presented together within a single narrative ethnography, focused on the character and process of the ethnographic dialogue" (69).

The Self/Other in Writing About Life

But we need more in order to acknowledge multicultural observers and observed. We need a fluid, process-oriented definition of ethnographers' roles based on feminist standpoint theories. Such a construct should include ideologies and complicate self-other relations in research. Instead of the standard participant observation or coparticipation, researchers should have a continuum of roles to play. Their role can vary from active involvement (more or less participation) to detached observation, the extent of which is decided by both the situation of natives and the researcher's shifting alliances with various ideologies.

I do not think these positions encourage us to be solipsists. They can help our research to be more objective with an ideological dimension. As Haraway (1991) claims, "Feminist objectivity is about limited location and situated knowledge, not about transcendence and splitting of subject and object" (190). Since no position can be innocent, science is intertwined with politics. We need a view from "somewhere" instead of "nowhere," so we should take into account the historical specificity of our own cultural subtexts, the unspoken hidden life that may disrupt the effect of what Geertz calls *the rhetoric of being there*. Whether it is an anthropologist who goes to an exotic culture, or a composition researcher who studies a more familiar classroom culture, the line between the self and other and between experience-near and experience-distant depends on the people involved.

All of us, however, have obligations to both the research community and the native in showing where we stand ideologically, because, as some feminist autobiography critics say, we must ask "Who is speaking? Who is writing?" (Morgan, 1991, 4). One reason is that many crucial issues in autobiography "take on a compelling 'other' dimension" (6) if we read women writers closely. If the researcher, like many women autobiographers, has a different sense of self, this "other dimension" should be discussed openly. Treated as "locations of uncertainty" (Nussbaum, 1989, xix) among conflicting ideologies, these other dimensions can sensitize us to more subtle cross-cultural differences, whether the culture under study is similar to or different from ours. We will then have sufficient space for discussing the dynamics of multicultural contexts, or various ethnoforces in research, so as to enhance our understanding of meaning making in ethnographic studies. This act implies blurring the boundaries between ethnographic and other kinds of cultural (life) writing like autobiography, biography, history, and literary criticism. In fact, ethnography is not just about others, nor is autobiography just about the self. In both genres, we write about "us" and "them" within the complex context of multicultural lived experiences.

Notes

1. For a detailed discussion of the appearance of the modern self in the West, see John O. Lyons' book *The Invention of the Self: The Hinge of Consciousness in the Eighteenth Century*.

2. Of the numerous postmodern efforts to demystify the self in autobiography, two articles are most influential: Sprinkler's "Fictions of the Self: The End of Autobiography," and de Man's "Autobiography as De-facement." For instance, de Man describes the autobiographer's self as a textual "trope" instead of a "real" or historical person. As for the concept of the "Other" in ethnography, see especially Khare, "The Other's Double—The Anthropologist's Bracketed Self: Notes on Cultural Representation and Privileged Discourse," and the essays collected in *Writing Culture: The Politics of Ethnography*, eds. Clifford and Marcus.

3. Mostly, this emphasis on textuality was derived from postmodern criticism. See note 2.

4. This issue is most clearly discussed in Smith's book *Discerning the Subject*.

5. For these alternative writings, see Bishop's "The Perils, Pleasures, and Process of Ethnographic Writing Research," Brodkey's, "Writing Ethnographic Narratives," and Van Maanen's *Tales of the Field: On Writing Ethnography*.

6. Later, I realized that my research resembled case studies more than a "pure" ethnography: it focused on some individuals instead of the writing environment. For differences between the two methods, see Janice Lauer and J. William Asher's *Composition Research: Empirical Designs*.

7. In *Appropriating Literacy: Writing and Reading in English as a Second Language* (29–31), Rodby criticizes the L2 writing community's attitude toward ESL students as based on the myth of Babel.

8. Due to my ignorance about the "Informed Consent" and the red tape through which I finally got my study approved, I had not given them the forms to fill out before I entered the field.

9. See Van Maanen, *Tales of the Field*.

10. For instance, Geoffrey A. Cross, in "Ethnographic Research in Business and Technical Writing: Between Extremes and Margins," warns us against the four extremes of "data-centered, thin description; subjects-centered groupthink; research community-centered groupthink; or researcher-centered solipsism" (118).

11. Many works discuss the influence of post-Romantic ideas of the self on composition studies. The most insightful, I believe, is Brodkey's article "Modernism and the Scene(s) of Writing."

12. A whole collection of essays by anthropologists, Jay Ruby's *A Crack in the Mirror: Reflexive Perspectives in Anthropology* deals with reflexivity. Its introduction connects reflexive thinking with the dual role of participant observation.

9

Describing the Cultures of the Classroom
Problems in Classroom Ethnography

Kay Losey

In the midst of my first ethnographic research project, I came to a startling realization: the classroom is not a single community nor does it have a single culture. This realization should not have surprised me. In fact, in retrospect it seems rather obvious. But because ethnographers generally study a single community, because a major tenet supporting microethnography is the assumption that the classroom is a self-contained community, and because so much research had already been done establishing "a general set of standards for how to act in school, a sort of American 'classroom culture'" (Shultz, Florio, and Erickson, 1982, 91) (see also Cazden, 1988; Mehan, 1979), I assumed that indeed the classroom had a single culture. Instead, I came to recognize that the classroom was composed of a number of smaller communities, each with its own culture. Obviously, there were teachers and students. There were also men and women. There were Mexican-Americans, Anglo-Americans, Portuguese-Americans, Asian-Americans. Some people spoke English as their first language. For others, English was their second or third language. The classroom I studied had a number of different communities with a number of different perspectives. In this chapter I will

This chapter has developed from my presentation at a roundtable on "Re-presenting the Classroom: The Tales We Tell of Teachers and Students" at the 1995 Conference on College Composition and Communication. Special thanks to Linda Flower, Joseph Harris, and Stephen North for their insightful questions and comments at the conference.

discuss the special problems the multiple communities of the classroom create in conducting classroom ethnographies. Using examples from my two-year microethnography of Mexican-American students and their Anglo-American composition teacher in a community college outreach program, I will explore the problems researchers face as they come to identify, understand, and describe the multiple communities of the classroom.

Many qualitative studies of the social context of composition instruction use a microethnographic approach called *classroom ethnography*. By definition, classroom ethnography is "the study of single classrooms abstracted as small societies" (Goetz and LeCompte, 1984, 23). In fact, Lutz (1981), in a chapter about how to do ethnography in schools, encourages ethnographers to take a cross-cultural perspective in which "a classroom may be observed as a cultural system, the school observed as a cultural system, and the school district and larger society may each be observed as cultural systems—all within the national culture" (60). Statements such as these perpetuate the notion that the classroom is indeed a single cultural entity.

It is not surprising then, that when I began my first classroom ethnography I therefore assumed only one community—the students'. Even when I collected data from the teacher, the counselor, and other relevant participants, my focus was always on understanding the students' perspectives, how they interacted, and why. Because I had assumed only one perspective, the teacher was able to most impressively and publicly correct my understanding of what happened in her classroom.

During my research project I organized a Conference on College Composition and Communication panel to present reports of ethnographic research at a variety of adult literacy sites. I presented my first preliminary data analysis after a year in the field. The paper described a case study of one student's interaction in the classroom and provided possible explanations for it.

I had a very good relationship with the teacher I was observing and invited her to be respondent for the panel. Because we were both busy—she, teaching four classes a semester at the community college, and I, teaching, visiting her class, and finishing up course work for the Ph.D.—we never had time to discuss our respective presentations. Like the rest of the panel members, I gave her my paper just a week before the conference so she would have time to prepare her response. And prepare she did! At the panel session she clearly and forcefully provided her perspective on what I had reported to the audience, taking all of the time allotted to the respondent (actually, she went over). She discussed none of the other papers. For nearly every explanation I had given regarding her classroom and her students, she gave an alternative interpretation. For example, when I pointed out that the case study student, Amado, had a lengthy history of writing failure of which the teacher had no prior knowledge, I assumed the teacher would have wanted this information to meet the needs of the student. The teacher, however, reminded listeners that given her schedule, she could not possibly spend the time to discover this information. Moreover, she did not want to learn it. She felt she would lose her objectivity toward her students if she knew about their past experiences, even past educational experience.

At this point I realized my mistake. I had believed that a single classroom community, composed only of students, could and did exist. Although a teacher myself, for some reason I believed that the teacher's perspective was unimportant. Perhaps I ignored the teacher's perspective because I was so close to it that I assumed I already knew it. Or, more likely, I ignored it because students, not teachers, were failing school in droves and I felt we needed to understand students so we could help them succeed.

Therefore, when I became a participant-observer I had focused on learning the students' opinions, their perspectives. I wanted to see the world as they did. But instead of being a single culture as so many assume, the classroom I studied was indeed full of people with differing group memberships and therefore differing cultures who were brought together in the classroom. Although the classroom has its own set of values, norms, and modes of interaction, those values and norms are imposed on the classroom, not agreed on by the whole (Heath 1982). If the classroom were really a single community, there would be significantly fewer misunderstandings and no communication mismatches. People would already have shared understandings of occurrences. This recognition is particularly ironic and potentially problematic because many of the mismatch studies, an approach that assumes multiple cultures, use classroom ethnography which assumes a homogeneous classroom culture.

Luckily, the teacher in my study did not kick me out of her classroom, so my research project continued. I was, however, left with a big problem: what does a classroom ethnographer do after realizing that there is not just one community but several communities to study, several perspectives on what occurs in the classroom, and several meanings brought to and taken from it? First, she needs to carefully identify those groups. Close observation within the classroom is an obvious must. Important, too, however, is observation outside the classroom. There have been numerous critiques of microethnographic methods because they often fail to consider important macrolevel information about institutions and the larger society (Heath, 1982; LeCompte and Preissle, 1993; Lutz, 1981). What microethnographers observe in the classroom does not occur in a vacuum but results from larger societal factors. From an anthropological perspective, formal schooling is but one aspect of socialization. As Heath (1982) notes, "The behaviors of pupils are ideally viewed not only in relation to fit or contrast with those of teacher, typical student, or successful pupil, but also with respect to home and community enculturation patterns of pupils and teachers" (37). Also, Ogbu (1982) raises a broader issue, namely that "the language, cognitive, motivation, and social competencies which parents and other childrearing agents seek to inculcate in the young—depend on historical and contemporary economic, social, and political realities of the population and not merely on the teaching competencies of its adult members"

(254). In order to understand the classroom, one needs to be familiar with the larger context. With regard to identifying groups in a classroom, remember that the school and the classroom do the bidding of the larger society. Issues of power, status, and dominant ideologies that are negotiated and circulated in the community and larger society are likely to be reflected in the classroom. The same groups that are in struggle in the larger society may well be in conflict on a smaller scale in the classroom.

Those who call for adding a macroethnographic dimension to educational microethnography (e.g., Ogbu) are right, in my opinion. In my project, I studied not only classroom and tutorial interaction and the personal histories of the teacher and selected students, but also data at the level of the institution and the community. At the community-college level, I was interested in how the services offered at the outreach program compared with those offered on the main campus and what bureaucratic constraints were placed on teachers and students. In the community, I was interested in which political, economic, and cultural issues were important in the past and present, which were silenced, which were given voice, and how those issues were negotiated. My study of these larger contexts surrounding the classroom revealed various groups in the community and their relative power and status. This information helped me to recognize and confirm the groups within the classroom and their relationships. I came to realize that the apparent teacher-student dichotomy I found in the classroom reflected other power-filled dichotomies in society, like Mexican-American vs. Anglo-American and native English speaker vs. English-as-a-second-language speaker.

After identifying the various communities within the classroom, the classroom ethnographer must decide how to proceed to understand her multifaceted community. She could continue to focus on understanding the perspective of only one culture in the classroom, such as the students, or she might try to understand all the communities she has identified. The decision to focus on only one perspective is often made in composition studies. Perhaps some of the researchers who make this choice have yet to realize the multitude of perspectives within the classroom. Others may feel more a member of—or more sympathetic toward—a particular group. They may have an acknowledged or unacknowledged critical stance that influences their decision (Brodkey, 1987a). Regardless of an ethnographer's motivations, focusing on a single community has its drawbacks.

Studying only one community and its culture provides an incomplete picture of the classroom and the context in which the understandings of the group are made. The interactions and understandings of the chosen group are created and perpetuated in interaction with other groups in the classroom. Studying the perspectives of all groups also yields greater insight into the meaning of what happens in the classroom. Imagine a court case in which only one side of the story is told—only the prosecution, no defense. No cross-examination, no independent witnesses. You certainly do not get the whole story. And you will not get the whole story of the classroom if you only listen to and attempt to understand the perspective of one group there.

Moreover, the classroom ethnographer who chooses to study one group often gets an unbalanced view of other groups. If students are the group selected, this approach may (and frequently does) lead to "teacher-bashing," or at least to taking sides, as if there were right and wrong understandings of what happens in the classroom. Of course, there are not. All perspectives in the classroom are legitimate, just different. When one takes the students' perspective, teachers often seem to be the cause of all their problems in and out of the classroom. My account of the teacher made during the presentation I discussed earlier made it seem as if it was the teacher's fault that she did not know the person in the case study's educational history and that somehow her knowing his history would remedy his current situation. In retrospect, that conclusion seems a bit simplistic. The student's situation was the result of his interaction with other aspects of the larger context, past and present, as well as with others in the classroom and his teacher.

On the other hand, if the teacher's community is the focus of a study that examines only one perspective, it may lead to a report that is tantamount to "blaming the victim," another problem in research that purports to take only one classroom perspective. When looked at only from the teacher's perspective, often students become the cause of every failed lesson, every misunderstanding; they create their own failure. Because I took the students' perspective in the Conference on College Composition and Communication presentation, my presentation showed the teacher in a less than favorable light. The presentation was unacceptable to the practitioner audience, but very acceptable to the research audience who accepted my desire to take the side of the "defenseless" student (who defends the teacher?). But my talk did not present the whole picture. I mentioned the teacher only four times in the talk. Three were short quotes to illustrate how little she understood the student in the case study. The fourth was a paragraph in which I presented how I believed she saw him, based on my observations and discussions with her. The rest of the eighteen-page manuscript was about the student.

Ethnographers who choose to study just one community in the classroom must also ask themselves if a single description or interpretation will hold for all of the individuals in that group. Although anthropology, like sociology, addresses the ways of a group of people, it is important to remember that groups are composed of individuals who are as various as they are many. We should not assume that the perspectives of most students or several students are the same or that all students have a single perspective. By selecting a small number of case study students, I was able to reveal the similarity and variability among the students even though the case study students were quite similar in that they were self-selected students who felt they needed help with their writing.

Rather than focusing on only one community, the researcher who has recognized multiple communities in the classroom might try to understand all those differing perspectives. This approach sounds like the perfect alternative, but it also has its problems.

First, how does one become a participant-observer in two or more communities simultaneously? It seems this feat would be necessary in order to undertake such an approach successfully. When you want to be a participant-observer of students and teachers, it seems possible as an observer, but what about the participant's part? Do you do the things the teacher does or those that the students do? With whom do you spend your spare time? Who do you talk with before class? Where do you sit? How do you behave during class activities? These are all considerations for someone studying multiple communities in the classroom. In my study, I attempted to understand both the teacher and the students, so I sat with the students during class and chatted with them during breaks in the three-hour-long class. But I usually talked to the teacher before and after class and did other "teacher-ly" behaviors like tutoring. So in being a participant in the teaching community, I compromised, to an unknown extent, my position as participant in the student community. By chatting with students during break and sitting in the back row with some of the most notorious students, I compromised my position in the teacher community. To what extent these problems related to studying multiple communities affected my role in and understanding of either community I do not know, but it is a factor of which researchers must be aware and of which they should make their audiences aware.

A better approach might be to engage a research team with each member responsible for studying a different community. A team of ethnographers might also help bring a range of expertise in the sociological, historical, political, and educational arenas to help interpret data from these varied perspectives.

Second, deciding to study all classroom communities inevitably leads the researcher to attempt making sense of the differing perspectives—resolving them in some way through an explanation. But this blatantly requires yet another perspective—the researcher's—a perspective colored by her under-standing of research and theory in the field and her own experiences in her own groups. The researcher's perspective does not have a natural place in the classroom and likely has little resonance for any of the groups in the classroom. It simply does not reflect the reality of any community in the classroom.

In a more recent write-up of the case study I mentioned earlier, I tried to use a more balanced approach in my presentation. I attempted to interpret from perspectives of both the teacher and student, but nevertheless everything was filtered through the eyes of the researcher. The student said he was a procrastinator. The teacher said he did not work hard enough. I disagreed with both of them and concluded that the student lacked experience in writing. Here the researcher's perspective does not reflect either of the participants' perspectives and yet was given prominence in the ethnography. I am not renouncing the conclusions of my work, but I do want to recognize that the interpretations made were mine, based on my own personal and professional experiences, and the same data might be interpreted very differently by someone else. Most importantly, the participants themselves saw it differently—and none of them can be wrong.

The less than satisfactory approaches to classroom ethnography that I have discussed here—focusing on just one perspective or attempting to resolve multiple perspectives—are likely choices in our field, in part because of our requirements for "good" educational research. Those in anthropology who are concerned with these issues lament the positivistic roots of that discipline (see Pratt 1986, for example), but the quantitative, positivistic history of educational research, with its foundations in psychology and its lingering suspicion of qualitative research (Goetz and LeCompte, 1984) surmounts that found in anthropology. For instance, many graduate schools of education refused to accept qualitative dissertations well into the 1980s. Moreover, research in education has a tradition of being applied rather than basic. As Bogdan and Biklen (1982) note, evaluation research, pedagogical research, and action research all "seek findings that can be used directly to make practical decisions about or improvements in programs and practices" (192). Such a disciplinary history makes it incumbent upon researchers to present a single "right" answer, some definitive explanation of what was observed. Ultimately only a single perspective—that of the researcher or her representation of one of the groups in the classroom—is acceptable. Moreover, that single perspective must be readily converted into practical suggestions for the classroom. But for much qualitative research, particularly that in the ethnographic tradition, such conclusions are inappropriate.

Whether one chooses to focus on a single community or multiple communities in the classroom, the problem of how to analyze and present data plagues today's ethnographer. The postmodern realization that the enthographer's representation of another culture's perspective cannot be devoid of the author's own background and personal perspective is the crux of the current debate in anthropological circles. Geertz (1973) identifies what many consider the problem (although *he* doesn't consider it so): "What we call our data are really our own constructions of other people's constructions of what they and their compatriots are up to" (9). And here Geertz is referring only to the ethnographer's data, his fieldnotes, not to his interpretation of that data. Traditionally, ethnographers have been concerned with finding the underlying meaning of what they observe and in presenting that meaning to their readers. Adding meaning to what is observed makes it what is called "thick description" (Geertz, 1973, 3). That sounds simple enough, but both the description and its interpretation are created not by the mythological objective scientist of yore, rather they are determined "contextually . . . rhetorically . . . institutionally . . . generically . . . politically . . . and historically . . . " (Clifford, 1986a, 6).

In order to find or give meaning to his observations, the ethnographer builds 1) an operational model—based on his empirical observations, 2) a representational model—from data from natives about their interpretation and meaning of what happened, and 3) an explanatory model—combining these two models with anthropological theory to create a model that "explains and predicts behavior within the culture under specified conditions" (Lutz 1981, 55). This last model is based on "the anthropologist's understanding of the representation and empirical models" (58). But traditionalists fail to recognize that this explanatory model is the ethnographer's perspective—just another point of view—not superior because of theory. And the ethnographer is at a definite disadvantage for understanding, compared with the natives themselves. That the ethnographer is bringing her experiences and beliefs to the initial construction of the data as well as their interpretation leads people to question the validity of a single interpretation or of any interpretation, period. Derrida (quoted in Herndl 1991) notes "whether he wants to or not. . .the ethnologist accepts into his discourse the premises of ethnocentrism at the very moment he is employed in denouncing them" (322). Despite the awareness of this problem that most ethnographers carry with them, in the traditional ethnographic genre "the ethnographer conventionally acknowledges the provisional nature of his interpretations. Yet he assumes a final interpretation—a definite reading" (Crapanzano 1986, 51).

Although many researchers in composition and education recognize the open debate in anthropology, which has led a call for new approaches to ethnographic writing, our institutions still show a marked preference for a single solution. I wonder if we need to have a single understanding of what is observed in a classroom. Is it always necessary to tie everything up into a neat explanation, especially since such explanations are often forced on observations by researchers who feel they must meet the conventions of their field? Can we learn also from representations of the classroom that reveal some ambiguity—from an awareness of the multiple perspectives that are at work in the classroom and how different they might be—and how difficult they are to make sense of?

Wolcott was ahead of his time in 1975 when he argued for ethnographic accounts that "contain a wealth of primary data," so that "readers have an adequate basis for rendering their own judgments concerning the analysis" (124). We need to accept attempts to reflect multiple realities in our micro-ethnographies. We should feel free to experiment with presentations that eliminate the single "right" interpretation as found in Western anthropological theory and the ideology it represents. According to Tyler (1986), postmodern ethnography "foregrounds dialogue as opposed to monologue, and emphasizes the cooperative and collaborative nature of the ethnographic situation in contrast to the ideology of the transcendental observer" (126). To him, "Polyphony is a means of perspectival relativity and is not just an evasion of authorial responsibility or a guilty excess of democracy" (127).

Although every attempt at a new method of ethnographic presentation will fail, as Tyler (1986) points out and many others indirectly suggest (see Herndl, for example), most anthropologists concerned with these issues agree that we should not throw up our hands in despair over the apparent Catch-22 in ethnography. Namely, we cannot extricate ourselves completely from our own cultural trappings to give a truly objective account of another culture. Instead, we should be forthcoming with our readers, admitting our limitations as researchers and, if giving an interpretation, call it what it is—a fiction (Clifford, 1986; North, 1987). Or at least call it just one reality—the author's.

Unless we accept changes in ethnographic writing to allow for the presentation of multiple perspectives, researchers will continue to be torn between the expectations of the academic community, which requires simple, singular conclusions and the real-life communities they observe and are a part of in the classroom, communities that rarely reveal themselves fully to the researcher or offer straightforward interpretations and conclusions. Of course, because professional acceptance and success are at risk, there will seldom be a lengthy debate about which community will be served—the academic or the classroom. The academic community alone will continue to be served and will alone reap the benefits of classroom ethnographies.

10

Between You and Me
Plotting the Contours of the Writing Conference

Marcy Taylor

The territory of ethnographic writing research seems so big and so
complicated, yet I know it is also arrived at with a simple map
because I attempted my own first project with no more than a nod
from my dissertation director, a few sociology and anthropology
field guides, and the understanding that this would be the only type
of research I would ever find comprehensible. (1994, 264)

Wendy Bishop

Although ethnography resolves none of these problems [of
subjectivity, of interdisciplinary, of social justice], it recognizes
them as problems. And, in so doing, ethnography creates the
preconditions for research and social responsibility, if only by
arguing that the worlds of words separating "us" from "them" are
not natural boundaries, but social borders that we help maintain
when we refuse to travel into uncharted territory. (1987, 42)

Linda Brodkey

All research tells a story, and as such it contains its own history—the tale of
its own making. This history, the story of the process and not just the product,
is often obscured in research as only the "outcomes" or "results" are

represented. While these results may tell a tale that contains some plot, it tends to squeeze out the settings (the "territor[ies]" Bishop refers to as "big and so complicated"), the actors, and the themes. And it is also a story which, as Brodkey argues, continues to construct academic discourse as a "world of words separating 'us' from 'them,' " literally reproducing through omission (or, as I would see it, a lack of imagination) an academic zone apart from the world in which real people live, work, and communicate.

Research stories—however they are constructed—are not the only ones we tell in academe. We also tell stories about our teaching. And our students, when given the chance, tell often radically different stories about their processes of learning in our classrooms. In fact, this chapter argues that one important way to approach an understanding of "academic culture" is through its narratives—complete with their own tropes, subjects, and plot lines.

For instance, like Bishop, I can tell the story of my history as an ethnographer of literacy. I entered the terrain of writing research as a graduate student, having read only a smattering of literacy/composition theory. I saw different groups of "researchers," each with very clear ways of distinguishing what constituted knowledge in his "field" of writing studies. Because I wanted to know more about students than about texts, and more about classrooms than about laboratories, I staked out a particular region of that territory for possible exploration. I started asking students what they did and what they thought as they wrote. I began to listen to their stories. Like Bishop, I found this region comprehensible.

This history explains, in part, how I have come to look into the stories we tell of and in our classrooms, and the ways in which ethnography can help us read them. In particular, I have chosen to focus on the discourse of the writing conference, one literate site which has become, in a sense, as familiar as a fairy tale through the myriad (re)descriptions of its shape. I look at conferences through this lens of cultural narratives. The rituals of schooling are encoded in familiar narratives; ethnography—as a form of dialogic literacy rooted in storytelling—can help us to interpret these narratives by focusing on the patterns, the plots, we have been socialized into through our schooling, our profession, and our positions in relation to students.

A Conferencing Story

One of the strengths of ethnography lies in its comparative stance.[1] To help me see my own conferencing narratives, I want to begin with a story which comes from Tobin's (1993) look at composition classrooms.[2]

> It is Michelle's third conference and she looks pleased. "I brought in a revision of that essay about my job at the grocery store. I think I'm about done with it. I think it's better than the last draft. I still might change a few things. I'm not really happy with some of the words I used and stuff. But

basically I think it's done. I think I'm going to start on my second essay this week." I read the introduction in silence . . . .

I am tempted just to tell her what is wrong, but I hesitate. I am aware that Michelle and I are not the only ones in this writing conference. Don Murray is here, reminding me that writers need the time and the encouragement to find their voices and their meaning (*Writer* 157). I hear Brannon and Knoblauch's argument about students' rights to their own texts. And I can't stop thinking about Ferguson McKay, whose case studies clearly demonstrate his thesis that "confidence is a writer's central need" (100). But there are other voices in the room as well: Thomas Carnicelli insists that I must accept my "professional obligation" (116) to give my opinion of each student essay; Pamela Richards argues that writers need to hear the truth because "the feeling that someone is humoring me [as a writer] is more damaging to my sense of self than outright attack" (118); and my colleagues, chairperson, dean, former teachers, and conscience all tell me that standards are important, that this draft needs to be revised, that Michelle has not pushed herself hard enough.

I finally speak: "So you are happier with this draft?" A nonquestion. I am still stalling. She has already told me that she is. But I want some time to think and I have learned that getting students to do the talking in these situations is essential. Often, when pushed just a little, students who claim to be finished with a draft will admit that the draft still needs work, that they still have questions and doubts, and, sometimes, that they even know what is wrong and how to fix it. But I have no such luck today.

"Yeah, I am." I wait to see if she will give up anything at all. Finally she asks directly, "Is it OK?" Her tone has changed now; she is sounding much less confident, aware that I am not satisfied.

"Well. . . ."

Damn. Why can't I ever let long silences remain? As soon as I answer one of my own questions, I always remember Graves' point about the value of silence and patience in writing conferences (99), but with a struggling student sitting there I often can't take it. I just keep thinking I have to get them, get us, over these uncomfortable moments. But that's the problem. Am I helping them by talking or helping me? (40–42)

How do we read such literacy narratives? As teachers of composition, I think we immediately identify with the "tensions" Tobin highlights as he wrestles with what to say and when to keep quiet. We can see the struggle between teacher roles that Elbow (1988) talks about in "Embracing Contraries in the Teaching Process," when he argues that "good teaching seems a struggle because it calls on skills or mentalities that are actually contrary to each other and thus tend to interfere with each other" (219). In Tobin's narrative, this clash of contraries is figured in his repetition of assertions followed by qualification: the familiar plot structure that says, "I want to feel this way, *but* I am also drawn in this direction," or "theory tells me one thing, *but* it also tells me another" that we use so frequently to describe our teaching lives.

So we have here a narrative of struggle—but with whom or what? And what are the stakes? We see a tension within the idea of process, given voice in the words of the composition ghosts inhabiting this passage: which way is the "right" way to act within this culture? This positioning within the rituals/rules of an educational system is also seen in the allusion to colleagues, chairs, deans, and former teachers who are looking in and requiring "standards." The addition of Tobin's reflections to the bare dialogue also suggests a ritualized response; although written in present tense as though we are witnessing the conversation, Tobin has contextualized his response. We are reminded of its *written* quality; it has become a piece of fiction rather than a transcript, an interpretation rather than the event itself. I will return to this idea of ritual and fictionalization, both so much a part of the writing conference and of an ethnographic "stance."

But isn't a conference first and foremost a dialogue between teacher and student? Isn't Tobin's struggle, in fact, to converse with what he describes as a "struggling student"? But *is* she struggling? When she enters the conference, she "looks pleased"; she thinks she is done. But Tobin knows she isn't. If he can just get her to talk, she will "admit that the draft still needs work." She may even "know what is wrong and how to fix it." Dialogue will bring her around—*to writing the paper he wants her to write.* His struggle to refrain from telling her directly what the paper looks like is only complicated by her point blank question, the one question we teachers *don't* want our students to ask in a conference: "Is it OK?" It is only at this point, I think, that Michelle becomes, for herself, and in a way contrary for us, a "struggling student."

This literacy narrative provides a certain kind of access into the cultures of composition studies, the profession of English, ourselves, and our students. I highlight "cultures" here because I want to claim that the ways in which we read stories like this—as examples of "successful" or "unsuccessful" conferences, for instance—depend on the ritualized ways of seeing and enacting composition (and, more generally, schooling) into which we are socialized as teachers and students. I also want to argue that ethnographically oriented research can provide a way into these cultures by explicitly and self-reflectively (de)constructing the stories of our educational institutions to reveal the contradictions that our tropes for literacy create.

Ethnography as Literacy: Reading/Writing the Map of Our Writing Conferences

As I mentioned earlier, process theories like those of Elbow and Tobin tend to figure these contradictions as functions of the "contraries" of teacher roles. However, these contraries exist not only in a struggle with the roles we perform as teachers, but in the clash between the *purposes* students and teachers assign to the activities of the writing course, a culture clash evident in the discourse of the writing conference. The writing conference becomes the site for examining the rituals of what we call "academic literacy."

Ritual serves as a powerful trope for interrogating the narratives of schooling. I am seeing ritual as Foucault (1972) does when he asserts that every educational system is the "ritualization of the word" (227); academic literacy becomes the ritual itself. Bourdieu (1967) makes a similar point when he argues that the patterns of thought and language transmitted by the school fulfill the same function as cultural creations such as rites or myths (339). Although the rituals of education are overdetermined, they should not be seen only in the sense of the repetition of prescribed conduct. McLaren, in *Schooling as Ritual Performance* (1986), argues that "as forms of enacted meaning, rituals enable social actors to frame, negotiate, and articulate their phenomenological existence as social, cultural, and moral beings" (48). I want you to consider the competing discourses of the writing conference in terms of ritual in that ritual implies *performance* (the actual patterns of speech and action negotiated between teacher and student during the conference—a negotiation I will show as "cross cultural") and *perception* (the expectations about roles/rules that students and teacher hold, which construct the discourse of the writing class).

This idea of negotiation and articulation suggests the metaphor of "dialogue" as central to the rituals of the writing conference. Regardless of whether approached from an expressivist or socio-cultural perspective, dialogue is a defining characteristic of process writing theories. Brodkey (1991) argues for a dialogic perspective on literacy that emphasizes the historical and cultural relativity of literate action within a given social site, such as a classroom.

One can see the urge toward dialogic literacy in Tobin's story, particularly in the sense of allowing writers the room to "find their voices and their meaning," and that students have "rights to their own texts." We also, however, see dialogue valued in a literal, instrumental sense: talk is good, silence "uncomfortable." But it is (always) the *student* who must do the talking: Tobin says, "I have learned that getting students to do the talking in these situations is essential." In this conversation, however, when the student speaks, she *does not* "admit the draft still needs work, that [she] even knows what it wrong and how to fix it." She asks directly, defiantly even, "Is it OK?"

If "dialogue" is one of our tropes for literacy, do students have others? Nelson (1995) reminds us that students are already long-standing members of the culture of school and are highly literate about how classrooms work. As Nelson argues,

> While it may sometimes be useful to see ourselves as insiders who can help initiate our students into the worlds of academic discourse, I believe that we may at the same time need to be initiated into our students' world, to position ourselves as outsiders to our students' interpretive practices in order to explore the structure of assumptions that guides students' choices when they write. (412)

Nelson highlights the need to "read our students' worlds" by reading our classrooms. Ethnography, including teacher-research, lets us do that by examining and creating stories specifically about the worlds our students and we inhabit.

In other words, Nelson's notion of reading student and classroom cultures as texts helps us see the tensions in Tobin's conference in terms of a sort of culture clash. Beginning college writers as a group occupy a distinct *cultural space* from that of their teachers. By virtue of their socialization *as students and teachers* through the systems of power in the schools, and by virtue of the differences in students' and teachers' relationship[5] to the activity of writing (and to the "work" of English studies), students and teachers construct interactions using different discourse systems that often work at cross (cultural) purposes.

Several ethnographies of crosscultural communication in educational settings have explored similar tensions. The most well-known are Heath's *Ways with Words* (1983), a study of language use in two working-class communities in the rural Southeast, and Philips' study, *The Invisible Culture* (1983), which specifically explores the ways differences in discourse structures serve to distance Anglo-American teachers from their Warm Springs Native-American students. Langer (1991) and McCollom (1991) also deal with crosscultural communication, specifically in schools. McCollum describes "tacitly learned discourse rules" that govern the interactions between teachers and students. She asserts that "cross-cultural comparisons of classroom discourse patterns demonstrate that participation strictures employed in each system represent different sets of rights and obligations that govern teachers and students during interactions" (111). Understanding the cultures of composition involves close reading of the systems of cultural ritual (and the languages used to participate within them) which students and teachers perform.

Let me give you an example from Brodkey's work in literacy education that illustrates these cultural oppositions, and the idea of reading a classroom for which Nelson argues. In her article, "On the Subjects of Class and Gender in 'The Literacy Letters'" (1989), Brodkey explores the development of correspondence between six white, middle-class teachers taking her graduate course on teaching basic writing, and six white, working-class women enrolled in an adult basic education course taught by one of her graduate students. This article focuses specifically on discursive subjectivity, primarily on the silencing of class distinctions through the use of educational discourse, which the graduate students used to enact the role of "teacher" and to assign the role of "student" to their correspondents. By analyzing the letters closely, Brodkey concludes that despite the fact that the teachers were "energetic and inventive practitioners committed to universal education," they ended up controlling the subjects of the letters by talking over or talking past their corespondents. Brodkey argues that this move toward silencing the students' personal concerns rests on a belief by the teachers—a belief which the students *did not* hold—that classroom language should try to transcend race, class, and gender. Like the conferencing stories I am telling, Brodkey's study reveals the clashes that occur when discourse systems collide, even when the goals of the interaction seem to be held in common.

Ritual and "Betweenness" Writing My Own Conferencing Story

During the winter quarter of 1993, I attempted such an ethnographic reading of my own classroom. Although I began my study with a very vague notion of what "academic literacy" means in terms of my purpose as a teacher, I focused on a rather bounded setting in which to explore this notion: the student/teacher conference. Ethnographies start with a sense of disjuncture with questions.[3] To frame my initial investigation, I began with the following general questions:

1. In what ways do students learn and use the "language" of writing?

2. How do the power dynamics of the one-on-one situation affect the kind of talk that occurs (in relation to the ways the students and I interact in the classroom)?

3. Are there differences in perceptions/attitudes (toward writing and toward conferencing) based on age, race, class, and/or gender?

4. In what ways does the conference as event help define our notions of literacy?

5. What do the patterns of talk between student and teacher reveal about the "culture" in which we both supposedly participate—the academic culture, the disciplinary culture, the classroom culture?

Through the various methods of data collection I used,[4] I became more narrowly interested in the implicit perceptions and agendas that manifested themselves through the interactions between my students and me in conference.

Brad[5] helped me construct one possible narrative of the literate behaviors of the writing conference. This particular story comes from my field notebook and describes the first conference I had with Brad, a senior forestry major enrolled in this 100-level composition course, his last writing requirement before graduating at the end of the spring quarter. Because I had audiotaped these conferences, this story is partially told through excerpts from the transcripts of that conference. We are discussing a draft of a paper Brad wrote explaining the ways a print advertisement makes a certain argument; Brad had written on an ad for Scotch.

> [Brad is more comfortable with participating than other students. He is very forceful in focusing attention on those aspects of the draft he wants to talk about. He sticks to his reading of the ad—questions me as to why I make the suggestions that I do. Seems a bit put upon (defensive?). But he is a senior—this is definitely a hurdle for him (a pain in the ass, if you asked him). He doesn't really see the need for revision; he is a good writer to begin with.

Puts me on the defensive a bit—no other students question *why* I am suggesting a certain change in their drafts. They don't question that revision is a good thing to try.]

M: Do you think this element, by itself, adds to the argument?

B: Well, I've noticed that in a lot of these ads they'll do the same trick. They'll have this picture that really isn't the product, and then they'll have the product on the corner—

M: Just so you know?

B: And so to me, what it's there for is obvious, you know, just so you know what the thing looks like. So I didn't think it was really worthy of any analysis, other than the color and the number of shot glasses.

M: Yeah . . . and that might be enough to separate it out, apart from the picture (pause)—I think you don't spend enough time on this.

B: Should I spend more time, are you saying?

M: I'm saying I think it should be a separate paragraph, probably.

B: Hmm.

[He really wants me to come to the point and *tell* him what I think he should do, and to justify that suggestion.]

M: So, separate that out as a category—I think that would be a good idea.

B: OK. What support do you have for that?

M: For thinking that's a good idea?

B: Yeah. Why would you think that this little picture over there would be worth more than I am giving it?

[I spend about five minutes explaining why—using terms like "organization" and "support" and the idea of strengthening his argument through development and coverage of all the ad elements, but I'm floundering. I'm not really all *that* sure that he needs a paragraph and I don't really want to *tell* him he does anyway. I am resentful that I have to justify my suggestion; I am defensive that he is questioning whether I know what I'm talking about. I feel somewhat intimidated by him because he's older, male, and obviously thinks this course is not worthwhile. After this long explanation, I tell him it's only a suggestion, after all. *He* needs to decide whether it "works" for him. He knew better. He ended up incorporating the change into his second draft.] (fieldnotes, 1/20/93; 1/25/93)

What happens when we try to read this story crossculturally, from the perspective of students' worlds? I interpret my students' responses in the conference setting to be indicative of their position *as students* in a setting, which in some ways is designed to transcend the traditional rules governing student behavior. The conferencing stories we teachers tend to tell ourselves are shaped by the ideal of free dialogue and the image of the empowered, active student "talking back"; but when they don't, we tend to interpret students either as "uninitiated" into academic rules of conduct—requiring a response from us—or as passive, as lazy, as wanting us to do all the work. But in the narrative above, Brad is certainly not passive, and I cannot say that he is a novice in the discursive operations of the university. He questions my suggestions, he takes the floor, he engages in dialogue. Why, then, should I feel angry and tense? Why did I feel this was a "bad" conference?

Brad operates under rules of efficiency and what I call "gradeability," and these rules include expectations about how to act within the rituals of schooling—including how to use teachers—for maximum effect. Undergirding student discourse systems is the belief that writing is the text itself, an imperfect product that becomes complete at the moment it is graded. This product focus may explain why fifteen out of sixteen students who responded to the survey I gave in conjunction with this project felt it would be useless to confer with me prior to writing a draft—as one student said, "It's better to write it out in an essay and see if that's correct." This focus on the tangible text contributes to the reticence many students feel about describing their revision plans in global terms; they tend to want to center conference discussions around discrete marginal comments I made to portions of their text. For instance, Brad focuses the discussion around one particular section of his draft, a section I had noted needed development. Our discussion of that section constituted over half of the conference. Although I had asked for development in other spots in the paper, this was the only place in which I suggested extensive revision, the creation of an entirely new paragraph. Brad's questioning, then, was designed to tease out exactly what I meant—and—exactly what I would accept. In other words, was I merely "suggesting," or was I, in fact, *telling* him that if he wanted a good grade, he had better change that section?

Brad's story is interesting primarily because although he exhibits many of the discourse features I found in the majority of my students that quarter—an emphasis on text and on correctness, seeing the conference as an efficient way to make a text gradeable—he is unapologetic, open, and very savvy about his role in the conference. As a form of literate action that has worked for him in college, he uses the conferencing rituals I have set up—for instance, the freedom to engage in confrontational dialogue—to make sure that I hold up my end of the contract in a dialogic literacy: that I will be completely clear about how I will grade his piece and that I will not ask him to do unnecessary work. I interpret his pushing me to clarify myself as a challenge to the very authority I assert over the reading of his text; it is a form of resistance to the literacy narrative that says that revision is always a necessary thing, that the instructor is always expert. The fact that I was a TA and he was a senior, I an English major, he a scientist, that I was female and he male, certainly contributed to our reactions (the power dynamic is very different in Tobin's story, for instance, where the student is female, the instructor a full-time male professor). Brad's demand that I define the criteria on which I judged his piece was based, in part, on a belief that writing was somehow completely subjective (as opposed to the sciences); the role of the conference, then, is to determine what *this particular teacher* "likes." In fact, in the survey responses, Brad described the purpose of a writing conference as follows: "To get an idea of what is expected for a certain assignment and to help us see things which we missed." In other words, if they miss something—if they misread me—the conference provides an efficient chance for them to re-read and re-make their piece so that it conforms. Success in a writing course means earning the highest grade possible given these constraints. As Nelson reminds us, "One of the most important features of academic work is that it takes place in a highly evaluative climate in which grades are exchanged for performance" (417). As a strategy for negotiating literacy within the university, Brad's "reading" of this conference was a success. He made the changes that earned him an A (and only those changes, which is, of course, also a version of successful revision).

I also want to suggest, however, that if I am able to read this conference from a position between Brad and me, between roles and the tropes we teachers have come to live by, I should also view this conference as a success.[6] Although I felt angry with Brad, my discomfort in this case came not from having a conference in which my student and I failed to approximate the ideal of dialogic literacy; it came from being confronted by a student who understood the possibilities of the rules very well.

We should not, then, be surprised, when students like Michelle ask "Is it OK?" And we should also not be surprised that we feel ill at ease, given our training in workshop pedagogy. But we should not blame students for our discomfort. Nelson draws on Doyle (1983) in arguing that "students attempt to manage the ambiguity and risk of academic tasks by focusing on the products they are required to produce instead of on the intellectual processes they are being asked to engage in" (417). Michelle and Brad were simply trying to manage the ambiguity. It is this ambiguity—the site of disjuncture between student and teacher cultures—that our ethnographies should explore.

Conclusion: Between Worlds

I want to end with one more literacy narrative, a story far removed from the composition classrooms I have been discussing as sites for research. It nevertheless illustrates the same kind of "disjuncture" of ethnographic interpretation we have seen in the previous two stories, the ways in which ethnography enacts the very struggles it studies: the problematics of subjectivity and self-reflexivity; power and resistance; scholarly authority; institutional codes and conventions; representation; and textuality. I give the story in full, as Clifford (1986) tells it, because it is, as he says, a "true parable":

> A student of African ethno-history is conducting field research in Gabon. He is concerned with the Mpongwe, a coastal group who, in the nineteeth century, were active in contacts with European traders and colonists. The "tribe" still exists, in the region of Libreville, and the ethno-historian has arranged to interview the current Mpongwe chief about traditional life, religious ritual, and so on. In preparation for his interview the researcher consults a compendium of local custom compiled in the early twentieth century by a Gavonese Christian and pioneering ethnographer, the

Abbe Raponda-Walker. Before meeting with the Mpongwe chief the ethnographer copies out a list of religious terms, institutions and concepts, recorded and defined by Raponda-Walker. The interview will follow this list, checking whether the customs persist, and if so, with what innovations. At first things go smoothly, with the interpretations of the terms suggested, or else noting that a practice has been abandoned. After a time, however, when the researcher asks about a particular word, the chief seems uncertain, knits his brows. "Just a moment," he says cheerfully, and disappears into his house to return with a copy of Raponda-Walker's compendium. For the rest of the interview the book lies open on his lap. (116)

This story argues that "both informant and researcher are readers and re-*writers* of a cultural invention" (Clifford, 1986, 116), making in essence the same argument Miller (1989) and Nelson (1995) make about our students' already politicized, rhetorical selves. It also exposes the dilemma (one might say the distinctly postmodern dilemma) of self-reflexivity and self-representation: the moments when the ethnographer—the hermeneut and rhetor—-becomes, in part, the object of his or her own interpretations. This parable about ethnographic fieldwork is also a story about writing studies, a lesson about how to read stories in the disjuncture between culture.

The tensions that now remain for me after such a re-reading of my conference with Brad are of a different sort than those I experienced while involved in it: they cause me to interrogate my root metaphors of ritual and dialogue; they force me to look at the ways performance and perception operate to create and to deny our students' and our stories. Brodkey (1991) argues that we all have tropes for literacy, but in our eagerness to instruct we teachers often cling stubbornly to our own and, like the teachers in "The Literacy Letters," we talk past our students. By reading our classrooms from a point *between*—positioned within the rituals of schooling but negotiating that positioning with and through our students' worlds—we can, as Brodkey says, "learn to read the unfamiliar tropes in which they write their lives" (167), and work toward mapping the unknown territories that lie between them and us.

Notes

1. Heath (1982) claims that one of the basic principles of operation under which an ethnographer works is that "[d]ata obtained from the study of pieces of the culture should be reacted to existing knowledge about other components of the whole of the culture or similar pieces studied in other cultures."

Ethnography, perhaps more than any other social science, strives for a comparative perspective. Research conducted in one social group should be accessible for comparison with that conducted on other social groups (35).

Or, in this case, we should carefully examine stories told of similar groups—first-year writing students and teachers of composition—in different institutions.

2. This story appears in Chapter 4, "Responding to Student Writing (I):

Productive Tension in the Writing Conference," in Tobin, L. (1993). *Writing Relationships: What Really Happens in the Composition Class*. Portsmouth, NH: Boynton/Cook.

3. In fact, I would argue that interpretive ethnography begins *and ends* in a sort of disjuncture. Brodkey (1987) argues that interpretive ethnography expresses "themes" that arise not from an intersection, but from a *disjuncture* between the ethnographer, the culture being studied, and the audience. The breakdown can only be mended, according to Agar (1982), through a dialectic process of questioning by which ethnographers construct an account of the situation (785)—in effect, inventing a story.

4. I constructed my study around the three sets of conferences which I conduct as part of the first-year writing course I taught at a large, state university in the Northwest. The course, English 131, is a composition course focusing on argumentative writing, and it fulfills a university writing requirement. I used a variety of qualitative data-gathering strategies, including participant-observation, recording of interpretive fieldnotes, audiotaping and transcribing of conference sessions, interviewing, surveying students using a written questionnaire, and eliciting evaluations of conferences through freewrites.

Although this process of data gathering and interpretation allowed me to construct an interpretation of my interactions with my students, even yielding an initial (and very different) draft of this article; I was bothered by the easy conclusions I drew. For instance, I relied very heavily on student self-reporting, particularly in response to the written questionnaires. At that point, I was more interested in what numbers could tell me about patterns of action. However, with the help of careful readers, I began to see the inadequacy of the survey design; it did not offer enough variety of responses and thus tended to lead students to answer in very particular ways. Likewise, it failed to allow the students to speak *in their own words* enough. Another systemic problem with conducting ethnographies of college classrooms is that the term ends too quickly, not allowing time for follow-up interviewing after spending time sifting through the data. This particular university is on quarter system, exacerbating the problem.

At that time, I also began to be more comfortable with the "written" quality of cultural accounts. I was making connections between interpretive ethnography as a theoretical construct and literacy. Through other ethnographically oriented projects on which I was working, I became more adept at "close reading, " that is, at finding the patterns of cultures in cases. I decided to turn from trying to *analyze* the conference event toward trying to *interpret* the story my experience was writing. (See Brodkey [1987] for her distinction between analytical and interpretive ethnography.) And so I put away the surveys, for the most part, and turned to the actual transcripts of our conversations and my representations of them in my field notebook.

5. Brad is a pseudonym.

6. I am suggesting a final metaphor for this story: a perspective of "betweenness," a term Kisten Hastrup (1992) uses to describe the unique reality of ethnographic fieldwork. She says, "It is not the unmediated word of 'others,' but the world *between* ourselves and others" (117). I am suggesting that we read our classrooms ethnographically, in this sense of mediating between our perspectives and those of all the "others" with whom we work.

11

Having Been There
The Second Ethnography and On

Wendy Bishop

I had thought . . . .that the process of becoming authoritative was much quicker than this. But then again, I was forgetting the lessons of process pedagogy. Just as I learned about the process of doing research and could now design a better ethnographic project, I am also learning about the process of writing it up. At least, [after completing my ethnographic dissertation] I will be somewhat more prepared with the stamina and determination required for a lengthy project next time.
—Donna Sewell (1995, 233–234).

Ethnography changes the ethnographer. Conducting a first ethnography changes our relationship to the field, to research methods, to our own authority, and, often, to our research subject(s). We're no longer the complete novice, and, as Donna Sewell explains, we're somewhat seasoned and certainly sobered. A naturalistically oriented writing researcher, after her first study is completed, not unexpectedly feels that she could do it better—next time. And there often seems to be a "next time" since many of us are drawn to ethnography because it *is* a complicated and compelling activity. As Paul Atkinson (1990) explains:

> The ethnography embeds and comments on the stories told by informants, investing them with a significance often beyond their mundane production. It includes the ethnographer's own accounts of incidents, "cases," and the like. They too are transformed and enhanced by their recontextualization in the ethnography itself. These narrative instances are collected and

juxtaposed in the text so that their meaning (sociological or anthropological significance) is implied by the ethnographer and reconstructed by the reader. (13)

In 1990, when I completed and published *Something Old, Something New: College Writing Teachers and Classroom Change,* a book-length study on the learning processes of teachers, I had just negotiated, to some degree, the complex issues of becoming an ethnographic writing researcher. This new writing research methodology demanded that I learn both how to *be there* in the field—entering a community, observing, participating, collecting data— and how to be *here* on the page (see Geertz, Works and Lives). After transcribing tapes, tabulating questionnaires, coding and analyzing journals, reviewing field notes, I had to create a believable authorial persona and prepare persuasive textualized accounts of my data and findings.

Ethnographic research methods were the most effective way of answering my research questions, the most theoretically sound way of studying the processes of writers, writing teachers and writing classrooms, and the most engaging use of skills I already possessed as a writer. For instance, the process of "textualizing" research data—that is, turning events into textual representations of those events—shared similarities with the methods of textualization taught in English literature departments and followed by creative writers who composed fictions and factions. Further, by completing an ethnography, I met several extrinsic goals, primarily, completing a Ph.D. in rhetoric and composition and being hired as an assistant professor of English.

When it came time to embark on "the second ethnography," another long-term study of college teachers, I felt well prepared, having learned the most basic lesson of research under the guidance of my major professor, Donald McAndrew: have a good plan (prospectus, outline, grant application, and so on) and the rest will follow. He taught me, and taught me well, that you can never improve a poor plan at the last minute. With Don's help, I created a workable plan and after the project was done I was hooked on ethnographic research; I wanted to go on because I agreed with Sonda Perl (1983) that such research provides rich (and personally and professionally profitable) tasks:

> [W]e view both writing and teaching as personal and social acts created by individuals within particular contexts. When we take this kind of approach to such complex phenomena, we don't end up with neat research designs, clear-cut boundaries and controlled variables. But we do find ourselves involved in an enormously rich task that often requires us to respond on a human level. (11)

Therefore, I began the second ethnography (Working Title: *Composing the New Teacher of College Writing*) following closely on the good plan of my first project. In my first study, I looked at experienced teachers as they returned to summer school to study theories of writing and teaching. In this study, I would be looking at new graduate teaching assistants beginning their graduate studies and training to be teachers for first time. Both groups were learning about writing theory and pedagogy but each group was at a different point in their professional careers and attending different schools under different time constraints. The difference in the two projects resided in the population and location of the school, then, but not in my data collection methods because I hadn't realized yet that new populations and locations might (probably *do*) require individualized data collection strategies.

Other problems arose. First, it was time for a project for this assistant professor on a tenure-line. Second, there were funding opportunities available. And third, that's what academics did, continued to research, as far as I could see. Luckily, I liked research and saw no problem with continuing. Although supported in-part by an NCTE research grant, and although all the data were collected according to plan, the second book-length ethnography, much to my regret, is still incomplete. Reams of collected data languish in blue plastic storage crates and I have published only one of many potential essays— "Attitudes and Expectations: How Theory in the Graduate Student (Teacher) Complicates the English Curriculum"—(with plans and personal commitment to a second) out of a wealth of data collected over fifteen months from gathered materials of eight case-study teachers' generously shared lives.

I realized—after data collection—that there were two major flaws in my second project. First, I had forgotten that the ethnographic moment is not replicable (evidence of this comes from my staying too close to my first project design, from not realizing that two groups of "teachers" could vary so much) since each investigation is created through the interactions of research design *and* researcher *and* community:

> This worldview [holistic, participative] sees human beings as cocreating their reality through participation: through their experience, their imagination and intuition, their thinking and their action (Heron, 1991). As Skolimowski (1992) puts it—"We always partake of what we describe"— (20), so our "reality" is a product of the dance between our individual and collective mind and "what is there," the amorphous primordial givenness of the universe. This participative worldview is at the heart of inquiry methodologies that emphasize participation as a core strategy. (Reason 1994, 324)

Second, by modeling this second investigation so strongly on my first, I became less engaged, more a technician, and less a participant-observer. I had moved my lens too slightly, focused too firmly, and did not allowed my project to breathe. I was more interested in the teachers as individuals (partly because they taught in a writing program I was about to become director) but less drawn into the project as a whole (partly because of my looming WPA apprenticeship). I knew (philosophically and methodologically) but did not understand (practically) the degree to which: "The ethnography is bound in time and place. The ethnography is uniquely shaped by the sensibilities and style of its individual author. The ethnographer is, we know, the 'research instrument' par excellence. The fieldwork is the product of a personal and biographical experience" (Atkinson, 29).

It was not until I had collected data and faced my writing-it-up responsibilities that I learned that I had overdetermined the outcome of my second major research experience. I did not see until then that I should have embarked on my second project for different reasons and in order to cover different territory by different means. I was exercising my skills but seldom reinventing and augmenting them. I had reversed the problem Mary Louise Pratt (1986) mentions when she complains about dull or poorly written research narratives. She asks: "For the lay person, such as myself, the main evidence of a problem is the simple fact that ethnographic writing tends to be surprisingly boring. How, one asks constantly, could such interesting people doing such interesting things produce such dull books?" (33). I had sabotaged my own work by making the "doing" itself dull. Data collection complete, my involvement in the project waned. At a growing distance from the intrinsic interest of interviewing human informants—real live teachers whose lives and work I was always interested in—I became too easily distracted by other projects. I found that I was not writing this research according to plan; I found that research was no longer a prospectus to dissertation proposition. Suddenly, I entertained the distractions of my new job and lacked the pressures of the job hunt that would send me back day after day to the data.

Certainly, too, during the time of this second ethnography, I moved toward other interests—writing classroom textbooks and conducting teacher–research and pursuing personal essay writing about literacy and education—and these multiple interests (which I couldn't afford to entertain during the dissertation process) seduced me from the time-consuming, sometimes tedious, work of writing up my research. Writing about ethnography overtook and surpassed writing *up* my second project data. Particularly since writing *about* could take place in essay- or chapter-sized chunks of writing time and those chunks could add up to enough understanding to compose a handbook (for instance, see *Ethnographic*, "I-Witnessing" and "The Perils," 1992). Also, writing *about* suddenly took on new importance as I began to teach research methods classes and direct dissertation projects. My line of writing followed my lines of immediate need.

Perhaps such developments might not have created such a guilt–filled year, when everything I wrote seemed to come at the "expense" of the "second project," if I had remembered some of my initial readings. For instance, in *Tales of the Field*, John Van Maanan (1988) mentions the tendency in anthropology for initial fieldwork to produce the same effect. For many, the anthropological ethnographic experience may still require three to five years in residency, but the ethnographic life thereafter often focuses on writing about issues in ethnography rather than on continued fieldwork since the researcher has often left the community (the anthropologist leaves the country and the classroom researcher leaves the class at term's end). When I first read this observation I was disturbed by it; now, I have experienced a similar trajectory. I began to teach research methods courses in ethnography, I began to read post-modern ethnographic theorists, I began to push the boundaries of methods and writing style in smaller-scale research projects. In that sense, I was more fully living the ethnographic life than I had earlier. Such a life was no longer "out there"—a project to be done for credentialing—but it was also "in here," all mixed up, part and parcel of my academic and writing life and I had to learn to accept and negotiate this new, seemingly boundary-less, existence. As Clandinin and Connelly (1994) put it, I was learning to live, tell, relive, and retell *my story*. This chapter, of course, is part of that process. Clandinin and Connelly claim:

> We imagine, therefore, that in the construction of narratives of experience, there is a reflexive relationship between living a life story, telling a life story, retelling a life story, and reliving a life story. As researchers, we are always engaged in living, telling, reliving, and retelling our own stories. (418)

Returning to *Tales of the Field,* I also find an argument that important research narratives had been left out of my training; rarely had I read about work that did not work, for rarely do we share our tales of research misfortune: "The implied story line of many a confessional tale is that of a fieldworker and a culture finding each other and, despite some initial spats and misunderstandings, in the end, making a match" (79). Clearly, researchers need to learn from their mistakes as much as any other learners do, as we encourage writers to do. And, equally clearly, they need to be telling problem stories as well as success stories; I consider my second ethnography a problem though not a failure—I failed to achieve full written closure though I certainly have learned much as I researched and as I contemplated the project. Still, it is rare for me to talk about my work as I am in this chapter, just as it is rare to read published reports of "projects where the research was presumably so personally disastrous to the fieldworker that the study was dropped or failed ever to find its way to publication" (79).

In this chapter, I am clearly sharing a confessional tale, but I don't completely agree with John Van Maanan that more honest confessions would uncover scores of disastrous, failed, dropped, or unpublished work. It might uncover—and fruitfully—some of this. But also, confessional tales provide accounts of the process of learning ethnographic practices and adapting to the ethnographic life, detailing researchers' adjustments, compromises, and confusions that inevitably occur in a first anything (that will of necessity occur in some degree in subsequent anythings, too).

Given this pocket history of one life in research, in the space that remains I want to offer as preliminary advice a few observations intended to improve life after the first ethnography. If the second ethnography is a continuation or elaboration of our journey and therefore part of our professional meditations, where might it take us and what do we need to do to make sure we arrive somewhere? To pose tentative answers to such a question, I'll look at four areas: goal-setting, learning from the process, understanding one's own research authority and direction(s), and accepting—for some this means embracing—the ethnographic life.

Intrinsic and Extrinsic Research Goals

It's crucial for the researcher to make professional goals personal goals, to merge extrinsic and intrinsic motivation. Ethnographic research is highly amenable to this strategy since what we learn in our work often improves our teaching, deepens our understanding of writers, encourages us to "read" educational settings more critically and carefully. While a researcher may be required in her job to conduct research, that same individual will probably benefit personally as a teacher by studying those issues that seem crucial to her. And, quite simply, to offer a good reading of our data we must find those data compelling, because the ethnographic process requires that we return to it again and again. If, in returning, we are not engaged, or if, because of design predictability or impoverishment, the return is tedious, we will not fare well. Therefore, to even attempt the ethnographic practice of creating an on-going "thick-description" of a culture the researcher must be engaged at all levels of meaning-making.

Ethnography offers narrative representations of how a researcher evokes a particular culture at a particular time. The ethnographic report is always several steps removed from the culture, being, as Thomas Schwandt (1994) points out, "an inquirer's construction of the constructions of the actors one studies" (118). Therefore, I think we'll find the culture and the construction-making most compelling when we have both private and professional commitments to making meaning out of the events we're cocreating with our ethnographic attention. For humanist—rather than social scientific—researchers, for writing program administrators wanting to know more about programs, for teachers eager to understand classrooms, for writers determined to learn more about writing—the intrinsic case study will seem preferable:

> In what we may call intrinsic case study, study is undertaken because one wants better understanding of this particular case. It is not undertaken primarily because the case represents other cases or because it illustrates a particular trait or problem, but because, in all its particularity and ordinariness, this case itself is of interest. (Stake, 1994, 237)

Finally, when undertaking the second ethnography, we are already more authoritative than we were in the first project. Now we may need to worry less about closeness to a culture (as when a graduate student studies a peer's classroom and has to determine/explore the degree prior friendship and assumptions about the teacher and classroom will influence the "scene of research") and more about guaranteeing our engagement and committing our time. This is probably best done by setting up intrinsic goals that are as strong or stronger than extrinsic goals. For instance, when applying for grant funding, as I did, making sure that a fundable research design doesn't overdetermine a project's direction (this is one explanation of what may have happened in my case).

To stay engaged with my data and my writing commitments, I've had to do as William Stafford suggests and "lower my standards" in order to begin at all. Instead of dreaming of a book that I'm not writing, I instead accept the value of producing an essay-length case study and working to understanding what I learn from the writing-up process. In doing this, I learn to accept the fact that I can't always produce products I facily promise.

Learning from the Process

Just as we learn a great deal about writing by the act of writing, whether our work sees the light of public print or not, we learn important lessons from the ethnographic research process—even when we need to let the data go or even when our final reports take an unexpected turn. This is a lesson I have to relearn with each project, large and small, and it's a lesson I see my students learning, and relearning. For instance, my data-collecting skills have improved through practice, while my second more frustrating experience led me to "study" ethnographic theory and philosophies and to question my own relationship to the method. The quote from Donna Sewell, which opens this chapter, shows the degree to which every new researcher reinvents insight(s) into the process. In research classes, my students and I have seen that short-term, miniethnographics can teach us a great deal: from what it's like to be stood up by informants to what it's like to enter a new culture, alone and insecurely.

Ethnographers learn from seeing, doing, being there and then being here on the page. Since they can't enter the stream of a particular culture in the same place twice, it stands to reason that they will constantly learn (and want to learn) from the process. Process writings, whether they show up in a final product in a manner now being undertaken by some post-modern ethnographers or in the form of intermediary texts that are later edited out of the final product, still, all, allow us to learn. Devan Cook, who recently completed her first ethnography that explores the lives of student writers who work, found herself including poems on how to be an ethnographer and personal narratives of her own work/writing life in the course of her many dissertation drafts. Some remain, some became texts on their own, circulating in literary journals, still others are now filed away. Steven North (1987) suggests we should expect to do this juggling of realities and genres given that ethnographers, as he sees it, are "Serving as a kind of alternate reality brokers, they [ethnographers] deliberately juxtapose one imaginative universe with another, struggling, in the effort, to make both more intelligible—to themselves, to us, to the inhabitants of those alternate universes" (279).

Research Authority Creates Research Direction(s)

The second entry to the field may represent the first time we truly feel professional. It becomes time to claim our membership in our research discourse community (particularly as we try to turn school-writing into journal or book-writing) and help (re)see the direction of our continuing research. For instance, in the five years since my first ethnography and now, my own movement toward more narrative reporting was confirmed by my wider readings in poststructural discussions that began in anthropology and are currently affecting the way we define ethnographic writing research. Learning about these discussions accelerated my move to cultivating an informal, narrative research writing style that allows me to investigate ethical, political, and writerly concerns more freely.

No one can give us a sense of authority. We must earn it *and* we must take it. The credentialing process of dissertation writing can only take us so far; reflection on our own position will take us another necessary part of the way. For instance, Sewell ended her dissertation with this meditation on authority and researcher roles:

> While I fully realize the main function of dissertations is to credential scholars, at times I managed to forget my probationary status, just as I did when I completed studying for preliminary examinations. During those times I felt most like a researcher and less like a novice. After the first two disorienting weeks in the "field," I could see the project coming together even as I struggled frantically to keep interview appointments and collect documents. Especially during that first summer, I was a researcher.
>
> Within the academic year, though, my roles became multi-layered again, as I was called upon to teach, mentor, serve on committees and do research; the next summer moved me back into a researcher role, but the role of researcher as writer, a new and scary one. And now, of course, in another academic year [as a new assistant professor], I am balancing mostly researcher and teacher [roles] again. (233)

Living (and Enjoying) the Ethnographic Life

Finally, completing the first ethnography and then going on, as a learning, fallible, yet engaged researcher, helped me realize that living (and enjoying) the ethnographic life overall is what I've really been learning about; and if the life fits, I'd say, wear it. As my initial research goals were achieved and then complicated by continuing research, I found my life in general has been enriched by thinking ethnographically. There are few things so pleasurable as participating in the imaginative and systematic thinking that an ethnographic stance requires. The drafting of texts also activates many writerly qualities and challenges that I value:

> [T]his issue, negotiating the passage from what one has been through "out there" to what one says "back here," is not psychological in character. It is

literary. It arises for anyone who adopts what one may call, in a serious pun, the I-witnessing approach to the construction of cultural descriptions. . . . To place the reach of your sensibility . . . at the center of your ethnography, is to pose for yourself a distinctive sort of textbuilding problem: rendering your account credible through rendering your person so. . . . To be a convincing "I-witness," one must, so it seems, first become a convincing "I." (Geertz, 1988, 78–79)

There is something very satisfying about working to become a convincing "I" although that I changes regularly. The I of my first ethnography has given way to the I of the second project who in turn engendered the I of this account. Each witness needed to be constructed, each journey taught me, and each continues to encourage me to travel on. Having been there and back again, I hope you'll allow yourself to learn from both failure and success, to be both idealistic and pragmatic as you embark on your research travels once again.

12

Ethnographic Dissertations
Understanding and Negotiating the Traps

Mara Casey, Kate Garretson,
Carol Peterson Haviland, and Neal Lerner

Graduate students in rhetoric and composition have become increasingly attracted to ethnographic approaches to theses and dissertations. Because of ethnography's narrative epistemology (Brodkey, 1987), new ways of representing human meaning in social life (Erickson, 1986), participatory story-making, and commitment to multiple perspectives, many graduate students see ethnographic studies as most likely to illuminate their research questions. However, even with what appears to be thorough preparation—taking research courses, reading example theses and dissertations, and attending carefully to the lore their classmates pass on—novice researchers still find themselves set back by a variety of theoretical, ethical, political, and practical dilemmas. What many students do not realize is that, as Frederick Erickson (1989) notes, ethnographers cannot eliminate the human dilemmas of field work and instead must live with them.

Because we believe that other graduate students and advisers can learn from our stories, we use this chapter to probe several issues that cluster around student-ethnographers' preparation, working landscapes, researcher roles, and adviser relationships. It draws upon our dissertation-writing and thesis/dissertation-reading experiences and is enriched by the questions and conversation of the participants in a 1995 Conference on College Composition and Communication roundtable (audiotaped with participants' consent) and a 1996 CCCC pre-convention workshop on qualitative research. Rather than attempt to give definitive answers to the dilemmas we describe, we share our stumbles, hoping that future student dissertators, their advisers, and their research participants will be better equipped to recognize and negotiate their own traps.

Time Is Money: Unanticipated Costs

Some of the greatest shocks to students, their families, and their advisers come over seemingly simple issues, such as the time required to complete ethnographic theses and dissertations. This work almost invariably exceeds even the most pessimistic time projections. Our collective experience is that doctoral students who elect ethnographic studies in composition and rhetoric generally spend at least one year longer than their cohorts who elect other research methodologies. Even more than literary or quantitative research, ethnographic studies must be allowed to follow "lives of their own." *Thick description* (Geertz, 1983) is rarely quick description; it demands that researchers follow tangents, which often generate the richest data but also consume extra months. Research questions splinter, multiply, hide, and more often generate more questions instead of answers. Audio- and videocassettes, piles of documents, and field notes accumulate and beckon for elusive interpretation. Drawing a line around the "pertinent" data is extraordinarily difficult, and one semester of data collection becomes two.

Wax (1980) observes that "the process of field work encourages growth and change in the investigators," so much that researchers often radically "alter their conceptualization of their discipline, of their projects, of themselves, and of their hosts" (276). We believe that this researcher growth is a valuable, even essential, element in ethnographic study, but its cost, particularly in terms of time, is considerable. Student ethnographers continue to observe, question, write, and revise while they watch their nonethnographer classmates graduate, find jobs, and move toward tenure. Over several months, students hear friends' and relatives' questions move from "When will you finish?" to "Aren't you done yet?" to simply awkward silences punctuated with comments about the weather. Certainly, as serious researchers, ethnographic dissertation writers must be willing—even eager—to invest heavily in their work, yet the comparatively greater time most ethnographic projects demand is a substantive issue.

Particularly when students are unprepared for it, this protracted dissertation time can create both personal and family problems, as Mara discovered during the three years she spent writing her dissertation. For her study of the meaning of collaborative writing to the students and teacher in a college composition classroom, she spent seven months writing the proposal, ten months collecting and preparing the data for analysis, and nineteen months writing the dissertation. Compounding the problem, her husband, supportive for five of her seven years in graduate school, reached the limits of his patience and tolerance. Not wanting this project to cost them their marriage, they both sought out therapists to help them get through this rocky period.

Another shock is the financial cost of an ethnographic dissertation. Audiotaping, videotaping, transcribing, and copying mountains of data can push precariously leveraged graduate students into economic collapse. Particularly for first-time ethnographers, the impulse to record, transcribe, and copy everything is a sound one, but it comes when their economic support is often thinnest—at the end of years of study when monthly checks to the therapist are nearly matched by those to the transcriber. A single study can easily consume several thousand dollars of recording and transcribing, in addition to the cost of renting or buying recorders and transcribing machines. Mara wishes that someone had warned her when she was designing her study that audiotaping every class session, conducting seven interviews with Shelley, the teacher whose classroom she studied, and interviewing each of the fifteen students in the class three times (at the beginning, middle, and end of the semester), would cost her about $3500 in transcription fees alone. With such warning, she could have modified her inquiry to involve more manageable taping and transcribing.

Power, Stance, and the Participant Observer

In addition to problems with time and money, ethnographic theses and dissertations almost inevitably challenge researchers' abilities to position themselves as "outsiders" to their research sites. This challenge comes about primarily because novice researchers, to ease difficulties with access, often choose research subjects and sites with which they are familiar. For example, Neal saw his ability to function as a participant-observer in the university writing center he was studying challenged by his position as senior tutor or "insider," who also had significant influence in the hiring and training of most of the tutoring staff. His role dilemma as a participant-observer was how to balance "participation in the lives of the people under study with maintenance of a professional distance" (Fetterman, 1989, 45). Neal was uneasy with the influence of his role on the representations of themselves offered by the writers and tutors whom he interviewed. Would tutors see him as an evaluative authority and represent their practice in glowing terms? Would students represent their use of the writing center as more positive or negative than was true because they felt Neal had the authority to evaluate and change the institution? As Elliot Mishler (1990) writes, "the account produced during the interview is a reconstruction of the past, shaped by the particular context of its telling" (427).

For Neal, the attempt to answer these questions meant building into his methodology the kinds of checks and balances that would ensure the validity of his work. For example, seeking multiple data sources for any one finding—comparing what tutors or students described in an interview as their roles in a tutoring session with actual practice as captured on audiotape and as described in written records—was essential to achieve "triangulation" (Delamont, 1992). As closely as he could, Neal attempted to follow the advice of Miles and Huberman (1984): "If you self-consciously set out to collect and double-check findings, using multiple sources and modes of evidence, the verification process will largely be built into the data-gathering process" (235).

While he tried to ensure the validity of his findings, Neal's position as both member of the group of writing tutors and researcher of those tutors complicated his relationship to his research participants. Although Neal assured his fellow tutors that his project was not "evaluative," that they had been hired because of their experience and abilities, practice under the intense scrutiny required in a qualitative study is never without flaws. After Neal was away from his research site and fully immersed in his collected data, he realized that what he was finding might not be as readily accepted by those he studied, particularly the director of the writing center who had created the conditions that resulted in many writing conferences becoming primarily a triage of students' texts rather than opportunities for students to learn.

Cassell (1980) notes that "Fieldwork, like friendship, requires a number of social lies to keep interaction flowing smoothly" (35). Although Neal did not find the need to commit "social lies" per se, his original intentions to share with his participants his findings and analysis were constantly challenged. During the year he spent gathering data, Neal chose to be open in sharing with his tutor colleagues the features of their practice he thought to be noteworthy, particularly the ways they established their roles in a tutoring conference and the ways they negotiated goals with students. However, sharing the transcripts of interviews, his field notes, and his preliminary descriptions of each tutor became sacrificed because of time constraints. Each attempt at inclusion and openness seemed to represent another delay in the arduous process of bringing a qualitative dissertation to a close. Ultimately, Neal found it essential to resign from tutoring in the writing center, creating a physical, if not psychological, distance from the site of his research.

Although Neal promised to share the written version of his findings, it was only after his final hearing that he could expose his work to the scrutiny of the tutors whom he studied. Once he did, the relationships he had developed with his colleagues over three years of working together did not crumble, but along the way he learned, as Stephen Ball (1990) describes, that "ethnography involves risk, uncertainty, and discomfort" (157). His closeness to his research site certainly magnified this anxiety, a state that perhaps could have been mitigated had he studied a writing center in which he was not an "insider."

Like Neal, Mara studied a familiar site: a freshman composition course in a university writing program in which she had once taught. To complicate the situation even further, Shelley, the instructor, was a fellow graduate student who had become a friend. Inspired by their reading of postmodern ethnography, particularly the work of James Clifford (1983, 1986), both Mara and Shelley believed that an ethnographic dissertation should, and could, be polyphonic. Mara planned, therefore, to have Shelley and her students respond to each draft of her dissertation chapters; however, Mara's adviser vetoed this idea, arguing that her study would never be finished. Mara reluctantly agreed to finish the study without Shelley's response, and she and Shelley planned to collaborate on a book reporting the study when they had both finished their dissertations. However, when Shelley saw the completed study of her classroom and decided that Mara had done a "hatchet" job on her and her teaching, both the friendship and the planned book collaboration ended.

Neither Mara nor Shelley anticipated the unhappy ending to their relationship because they did not know about Wax's (1980) warning that "neither party can be sure of what will be entailed by the course of the fieldwork" (282). Although she did not realize she was doing so at the time, Mara, a teacher herself, quite naturally tended to view the classroom through the teacher's eyes during collecting the data for her study. After Mara was away from the field, she was facing the mounds of multiple data sources and subjecting them to close analysis not normally available to participants living from moment to moment in the classroom. At that point Mara began to see a different picture from the one Shelley and her students saw from their perspectives as participants.

Even if relationships can be successfully negotiated during the data collection phase of the study, as Mara and Neal felt theirs were, participants may be unhappy with the way they find themselves represented when the research report is finally written. Research participants are functioning in a hierarchical situation, one in which the researcher has most of the power to tell their stories. The saying that "No man is a hero to his valet" can be paraphrased, "No subject is a hero to the ethnographer—nor an ethnographer to the subject," says Mara. Concluding that it was inevitable that Shelley would reject her interpretation of the meaning of collaborative writing in her classroom, Mara wishes that they both had read Thorne's (1980) observation that the ambiguities in the researchers-subject relationship "make it easier for one's subjects to forget they are subjects, to think of the researcher *only* as a friend" (291). Urging students not to study spouses or partners, prospective employers, colleagues, or important friends and their sites, Mara and Neal propose that the possibility of conflict over observations and interpretations is likely to compromise either the study or the relationships or both, risks that can even end academic careers or relationships.

Even if Shelley and her students had been able to collaborate on each of Mara's chapters, Clifford (1983) suggests that multiple-authored works seem to need an executive editor. As we write now, after completing our dissertations, we want to resist Clifford's suggestion in favor of carefully negotiated collaboration, but we see the pertinence of his observation to many dissertation-writing situations. Because, as Clifford (1986) indicates, all readings are contingent, historical, and contested, no two writers will read a culture in the same way or "from a neutral or final position" (18). However, collaborating authors can represent their differences more easily in texts that are not the currently required *monovocal* "school writing" of dissertations or in writing situations in which one of the authors is not being represented or judged by the other.

Mara now believes that it is impossible to disperse ethnographic authority. Institutional constraints and political inequalities work to silence multiple voices, and ethnographic dissertators, like quantitative researchers, will always write of others as if they were discrete objects or texts. A sense of mutual betrayal will always haunt writers and their subjects as they continue to use each other for their individual purposes. Janet Malcolm's (1989) description of the journalist-subject relationship seems to apply to the relationship between ethnographers and their participants: "The writer ultimately tires of the subject's self-serving story, and substitutes a story of his own. The story of subject and writer is the Scheherazade story with a bad ending: in almost no case does the subject manage to, as it were, save himself" (46). Neither does the ethnographer.

One discussion during a workshop at the 1996 CCCC on the challenges of turning qualitative data into written text illustrates the possible risks of written representations. As discussants began to consider how much detail from an interview transcript should be included in a dissertation, they readily saw competing needs. As ethnographers, they valued the thick description essential to a solid study; however, they also recognized the danger those details boded for the participants, two graduate-student teaching assistants criticizing the composition program in which they worked. Although the teachers would be described under a pseudonym, dissertation advisers would certainly recognize the participants, and those graduate students' careers were likely to be jeopardized. To warn all potential research subjects of any possible negative outcomes would be impossible, but even if such outcomes could be anticipated, the value of scholarship would be limited, for it would restrict participants to a very small group of persons with "nothing left to lose."

Given this tangled researcher-subject relationship in ethnographic research, informed consent poses slippery questions. How can subjects in studies that are emergent in nature be fully informed participants in research that will predictably take unpredictable turns? The answer is that they cannot be fully informed because "both risks and benefits (especially long-term ones) are often difficult to assess, especially at the beginning of a field study" (Thorne, 1980, 285). In addition to the difficulty of informing subjects of unknown findings and consequences, ethnographers-in-training are likely to study vulnerable subjects, such as students, whose participation is often decided by classroom teachers or program directors. Yet, not to disclose risks as fully as possible is unethical; this impasse remains a substantive dilemma for our field.

Knowledge Construction—Interpretive Challenges

After students have negotiated issues of access and consent and strike out into the thicket of the ethnographic field, it is not without guides to the terrain and what to expect. Trailblazers seem, in fact, to come in pairs, such as Glaser and Strauss (1967), Bogdan and Biklen (1992), Miles and Huberman (1984), Lincoln and Guba (1985), and Athanases and Heath (1995); they offer elaborate directions for how to proceed, gather data, and interpret findings. They urge students to develop grounded theory through persistent hypothesis testing and confirmation checks, assuring them that unifying concepts will emerge from the data as they develop explanations that account for events and continually seek disconfirming as well as confirming evidence back out in the field (Glaser and Strauss, 1967). However, no matter how often novices are warned that "data gathering and data analysis form the problem statement, just as the [problem] statement informs the data gathering" (Wolcott, 1990, 32), it remains difficult, before the fact of actual fieldwork, for student-researchers to appreciate fully what a "no-ethnographer's-land" these continually shifting sands can feel like. There is a great distance between the orderliness implied by much of the literature that describes "method" and the unpredictability of the process itself.

Novice ethnographers receive, for example, very little help in defining a problem: "Most textbooks on ethnography implicitly begin once the research site and general approach have been identified. The "pre-history" of the research is almost always invisible" (Atkinson, 1992, 4). Students are thus left to try to imagine the kinds of studies they would like to do, with very little to go on save the finished products of others. Unlike literary studies, there is a seemingly limitless source of data, and the sheer scale of the enterprise can be overwhelming. For example, at first, Kate wanted to study teacher beliefs. In addition to looking at reflective teaching logs and other personal writing, she felt she needed to study the institutional framework in which each teacher worked. She also needed to compare beliefs with actual classroom practice, and then she needed to place the various models that emerged within a theoretical context defined by both linguistic theory and the pedagogical literature. She studied three sites, three teachers, and three very different academic programs. She asked whether she should include students' views. How much student work should she review? Defining the boundaries and parameters of the inquiry was not easy; nevertheless, the novice ethnographer hopes to capture it all through the sheer volume of data collected. Kate often felt that she might be caught in "the inherent trap [of the] boundless freedom of an inadequately focused descriptive study" (Wolcott, 1990, 36). Although it is not possible to circumscribe the subject of study fully in advance, Wolcott (1990) believes that dissertation committees need to provide firm guidance in these matters in the interests of limiting the time spent in doctoral apprenticeship. Carol recounts gratefully her adviser's willingness to at least occasionally pair her exhortations about the dissertation's importance with a reminder that it also was a prelude to an even more satisfying post-dissertation scholarly life.

The process of making sense in writing of rich but overwhelming data is also one of the least discussed aspects of qualitative research:

> The process whereby complex and often confusing arrays of "data" are transformed into written accounts is often taken for granted. The inexperienced ethnographer might be forgiven for thinking that any problems encountered in that activity reflected merely his or her personal failings. (Atkinson, 1992, 4)

Both the early problem setting and the later writing of ethnography "rest squarely within, and depend heavily upon, textual traditions and acts of reading and writing" (Atkinson, 1992, 6). This epistemology means that novice researchers may place their studies within the framework of similar texts; for example, Kate admired the textured qualities of the teacher-thinking literature and its valuing of pedagogical practice and identified Sondra Perl and Nancy Wilson's *Through Teachers' Eyes* as a possible model. At the same time, she admired Britzman's (1991) *Practice Makes Practice* and Edelsky's (1991) *With Literacy and Justice for All* for their identification of larger social problems and contradictions. However, when we say that ethnography is defined centrally by its participation in acts of reading and writing, we mean far more than a choice of method, scope, or final written form. If perception itself is mediated by the kinds of stories that can be told, then it becomes important to deconstruct the textual tradition. This critical analysis of classroom studies was not generally part of our ethnographic training, but perhaps it should have been. Such study would give the novice a better sense of the inner workings of the craft, including the implications of various representational strategies.

Kate found being conscious of her own arsenal of potential narrative strategies was particularly enabling when she was writing her case studies of the three teachers' approaches to language teaching. Instead of charting similarities and differences across cases by using uniform categories, she employed figurative language that fit the separate sites and issues. In writing the first case study, for example, she used the metaphor of an orchestra conductor to capture an essential dimension of the teacher's conception of her role. However, in writing the second, the spatial metaphors of contact zones, safe houses, and disciplinary boundaries as they have been developed in the composition literature (Pratt, 1991; Bizzell, 1994) provided the conceptual framework for discussion. In the third, an altogether different metaphor was used, the concept of "layerings" in belief systems. When she made the decision to represent her cases in this way, Kate was not sure the approach would be acceptable, and in a less innovative academic setting, it might well not have been. These, too, are unsettled issues for us as a field, and they are connected to how we view our knowledge construction.

Of course, the transformation of "data" into a written account is problematic for all writers. It has been said that "an abyss lies between the writer's experience of being out in the world talking to people, and her experience of being alone in a room writing" (Malcolm, 1989, 72). As Mara and Neal noted earlier, the roles and stances that an ethnographer adopts while researching may radically differ from the roles and stances that emerge while writing. This is in part because the intense scrutiny of data coupled with multiple perspectives on a question guarantee a reading of the situation different from the perspectives in the field. Furthermore, observing in social settings and talking with participants create challenges and pleasures that are different in kind from those of interpretation and representation in the construction of an ethnographic account. The kind of person drawn to the interactive, social world of fieldwork may even find the habits of mind and isolation required of the analyzer to be an anathema. Although she enjoyed her field work, as she faced her thirty-two binders of data day after day, Mara often felt as though she were trying to turn straw into gold, with no Rumpelstiltskin around to ease her isolation and confusion.

Kate was also at times overwhelmed by the sameness of the terrain, dotted as it seemed to be with very similar individual entities. Broad pedagogical categories, such as transmission and transactional models of language teaching, for example, seemed to limit what could be said to the depressing and trite. Her sense of a possible forest was overwhelming the individual trees. At other times, the sheer individuality of each instance seemed to defy a sense of any whole. At these moments, she felt that each pedagogical practice possessed so much unique and local color that any attempt to establish comparable terms would destroy the practice's richness and interest. Case #1 seemed to have little in common with case #2, and the whole project seemed ill-conceived and ill-defined. Kate found herself asking, "What was that question, again?" (Ely, 1991, 54)—the trees were overwhelming her sense of the forest. Discovering categories to describe each case in a meaningful way involved more interaction with her constructed data. But most of all, it required the leap of faith necessary to all writing. It is difficult for student ethnographers to trust that, with time and the work of making sense, whichever path they take through the woods will lead them somewhere useful.

Dialogue with the Authorities: Whose Voice?

In addition to uncharted and contradictory relationships with their subjects and their data, ethnographers-in-training struggle through uncharted and contradictory relationships with readers and advisers. In fact, the student-adviser relationship, a relationship that most students expect to be a primary support, is in ethnographic research particularly sticky and complex for at least three reasons.

First, many decisions cannot be made until after students embark on their studies. The decisions shape the studies, so they are important, yet students must make them quickly and without consultation. Advisors and students who are accustomed to interrogating literary texts or constructing quantitative study protocols and analyzing the data that emerge are more likely to be able to project the course of their studies from the outset, confident that while their readings, discoveries, or results may be surprising, the studies themselves will follow familiar courses. In contrast, ethnographic studies have less predictable lives of their own. They require ongoing and extended decision making, often in the field in the adviser's absence.

Although this feature of ethnographic study will not go away, advisers can help students greet them confidently and competently. They can prepare students for in-field decision making, even "dry-running" some of the possibilities. As they help students second-guess those decisions, they can limit the number they see as fatal, they can help students understand the decision-making factors they might consider another time, and they can allow even retrospectively poor decisions to inform studies in useful ways. Carol notes, for example, her adviser's willingness to describe her own fears as she had to decide when already observing in a classroom how to move a single microphone to best represent the class discussion. When Carol then faced similar on-the-spot decisions, she was not paralyzed; she knew how to think quickly and flexibly, confident that her theoretically informed judgments would not be fatal and that even if they were not first rate, she could learn from them.

Second, student-researchers are the chief observers-interviewers, and thus they make decisions about what data they "see" and what interpretive frames they select, a process that irretrievably shapes the data before advisers can intervene. When student and adviser puzzle together over the transcript of a videotape, they already are studying an interpretation of an interpretation rather than primary data. This relationship to the data complicates traditional adviser-student roles in that it is more difficult for advisers to guide the research or to offer explicit suggestions. Whereas advisers of literary or quantitative studies can take fairly firm positions on the appropriateness of theoretical and interpretive approaches or of statistical procedures, advisers of ethnographic studies are particularly reluctant to "tell students what to do." This is tied partly to their recognition that only the primary participant-observer can "know what to do" and partly to ethnographic researchers' reluctance to chart the course for another.

However, this respect for researcher-knowledge often is coupled with a firm sense of what qualifies as substantive and appropriate research, particularly when advisers anticipate signing their names to the finished studies. This process frequently leaves students even more enmeshed in the guessing game of "I won't tell you what to do, but I expect that you will conform to my unstated expectations." Through the trial and error of this guessing game, Mara learned that although there is no "right" way to write an ethnographic dissertation, there certainly seemed to be many "wrong" ways.

Both advisers and students can contribute here by foregrounding the research questions and by being candid about what is and is not negotiable. Rather than sending advisees off to stew in their bewilderment, assuming that they either must not have asked good questions or not heard the answers, advisers can sketch the dilemmas. They can show why direct advice, which students may resent but at least are able to follow, is elusive in ethnographic studies. They can also help students create decision-making frameworks that will generate answers both of them can live with. For example, when Carol and her adviser were at odds over how to frame the differences between disciplinary and pedagogical discourse communities, they discussed several options. Her adviser then set out the parameters within which Carol could make her choices. Thus, the mentor can maintain integrity without dictating choice that should be the ethnographer's own.

Finally, many ethnographic studies are conducted in the margins or intersections of several disciplines or departments: literature, composition, rhetoric, linguistics, education, cultural studies, sociology, and psychology, for example. These locations allow students and advisers to converge in fruitful ways, but they also set the stage for conflicts. Carol offers her study of writing-across-the-curriculum communities as an ironic example: even as she and her adviser puzzled through ways of understanding faculty members' disciplinary and pedagogical differences as they approached student writing, Carol and her adviser also often talked past each other, one coming to the study from composition and literary theory and the other from English studies and curriculum. Although they both agreed that their conflicts opened instructive gaps, these gaps also created significant frustration for both of them.

However, they both discovered that engaging all of the situation-reading skills they possessed as ethnographers in the field allowed them to be both more candid and more diplomatic as they interacted with each other in the adviser's office. Carol says that she now tries to incorporate what she learned from these difficult but instructive interactions to her own conferences with advisees. "For example," she says, "sometimes when students seem not to understand something that I think they should know already and that I've just explained again in exquisite detail, I want to blurt out, "How could you have taken three contemporary theory courses and still not know this?" However, when I use the situation-reading skills I apply when I'm studying in a field, I know that my jab is grounded half in my own feelings of inadequacy as an adviser and as the instructor of those courses. I also see that venting my frustration will only make the student want to retort, 'Beats me; you taught those courses and you gave me A's—why can't I?' When I read our interaction thoughtfully, I can instead offer, 'The concept we are working on is difficult, and I'm feeling a little inadequate because I can't get us unstuck. You also may feel awkward because I keep intimating that you should already know this. Let's try to wade through this thicket together without worrying about whether either one of us looks stupid. The important outcome is that you leave here knowing what you want to do next, not just guessing or feeling battered.' Using the listening and interpretive skills we have honed regularly in our ethnographic work can help us interpret each other constructively," Carol concludes.

Even when advisers and students skillfully negotiate the complexities of their relationship, their most difficult task will be creating and responding to the text in the long, slow process of producing an ethnographic thesis or dissertation. This process will be less traumatic, however, if they both expect that the student's early drafts will be fuzzy and disappointing. Advisors can encourage their students to keep writing by finding something—anything!—positive to say about early efforts, helping students discover what they are trying to say, and trusting that eventually the report will turn out the way they both want it to be; to this end, it is important for advisers to focus on content before form and to tackle big problems first, one problem at a time. If advisers try to correct all of the problems at once in early drafts, as Mara's adviser did, the student has no choice but to ignore most of the feedback because it is too overwhelming and too discouraging. This, of course, makes the process even more tedious and frustrating for all concerned.

Perhaps professional writing teachers should not need our advice, but while many may "know" approaches for responding to texts-in-progress, the complexities of the dissertator/adviser relationship that we have experienced can lead to inconsistent application of such techniques. Similarly, student-dissertators might simply develop a "thick skin" in the face of a barrage of criticism from their advisers, but this protective layer can lead dissertation writers to become equally insensitive, ignoring good writing teaching practices that their advisers modeled. A rapprochement would include sensitivity to these issues and the realization that the ultimate goal is not merely a completed dissertation, but one that reflects well on the reputation of the major adviser and the writer.

Free at Last

The traps we have detailed and the routes student ethnographers and their advisers can take to avoid them are consistent with ethnographic epistemology. They hang on careful readings of participants' language and texts and on participatory story-making; they rely on collaborative inquiry, on multiple perspectives, and they honor the local as well as the global. As a result of our experiences, we are all committed to the pursuit of ethnographic research in a variety of settings, and none would have chosen a different method.

Elliot Eisner (1991) describes the goal of an ethnographic account as a kind of "guide" for the reader:

> Guides call to our attention aspects of the situation or place we might otherwise miss. They are typically prepared by people who have visited a place before and know a great deal about it. If the guide is useful, we are likely to experience what we otherwise might have missed, and we may understand more than we would have without benefit of the guide. The good guide deepens and broadens our experience and helps us to understand what we are looking at. (59)

Our wish in this chapter is to provide readers with a guide to managing the very real challenges of pursuing ethnographic theses and dissertations. Guides do not eliminate all frustration or missteps, but they can promote the confidence student ethnographers need to wade into their studies, make midstream decisions, and work productively with faculty advisers. In addition to helping students emerge successfully from the dissertation process, guides can nurture the competence and enthusiasm of new researchers—and of the students they soon will advise—for further ethnographic scholarship.

Contributors

Wendy Bishop teaches writing at Florida State University. She is the author of *Something Old, Something New: College Writing Teachers and Classroom Change, Released into Language: Options for Teaching Creative Writing,* editor of *The Subject Is Writing* and co-editor, with Hans Ostrom, of *Colors of a Different Horse: Rethinking Creative Writing, Theory and Pedagogy.* Her forthcoming books include *Thirteen Ways of Looking for a Poem* and *Metro: A Guide to Writing Creatively* (co-authored with Hans Ostrom and Katharine Haake) from Longman, *Teaching Lives: Essays and Stories* from Utah State University Press, and *Ethnographic Writing Research* from Boynton/Cook Heinemann.

Richard Blot is an Assistant Professor at Herbert H. Lehman College (CUNY) where he focuses on cultural anthropology, sociolinguistics as well as the anthropology of learning and literacy. He is editor of *Language and Social Identity* (forthcoming from Gordon and Breach), and *Foundations of Anthropology and Education* with J. Niehaus and R. Schmertzing (forthcoming from Bergin and Garvey). He has published articles and book chapters in *TESOL Quarterly, American Anthropologist,* and *Anthropology and Education Quarterly.*

H. Eric Branscomb is Coordinator of Basic Writing, Salem State College, Salem, Massachusetts. In addition to basic writing and ethnographic research, his professional interests are computers and hypertext, Lev Vygotsky and psycholinguistics, and the history of the English language. He has presented papers at CCCC and NCTE as well as a variety of other conferences, and he has published in the *Journal of Teaching Writing, College English, Journal of Popular Culture,* and *Writing Center Journal.*

Robert Brooke teaches composition, critical theory, and English education at the University of Nebraska-Lincoln, where he directs the Nebraska Writing Project. In addition to his Braddock-Award winning article "Underlife and Writing Instruction," Brooke has published three books based on ethnographic participant-observation studies: *Audience Expectations and Teacher Demands* (with John Hendricks), *Writing and Sense of Self,* and *Small Groups in Writing Workshops* (with Ruth Mirtz and Rick Evans).

Mara Casey (University of California, Riverside, Ph.D.) teaches in the Writing and Reading Center at Longbeach City College. She is coeditor of *Children's Voices: Children Talk About Literacy* (Boynton/Cook 1993). Her ethnographic works include a study of the meaning of collaborative writing in a college composition class, and she is currently working on a longitudinal study involving phenomenological interviewing of students' and teachers' changing attitudes toward writing from third to twelfth grade. She is cofounder of CCCC's special interest group in qualitative research.

Geoffrey A. Cross is Associate Professor of English at the University of Louisville, where he teaches in the doctoral program in rhetoric and composition and coordinates the writing-across-the-curriculum program. He has published a book-length ethnography, *Collaboration and Conflict* (NCTE award for best book in Scientific and Technical Writing for 1995). His articles have been published in *Research in the Teaching of English, Computers and Composition,* and *The Journal of Business and Technical Writing,* along with a chapter in the NCTE-award-winning *Writing in the Workplace: New Research Perspectives* (Ed. R. Spilka. 1993: Southern Illinois University Press). Currently, he is working on a grant-funded ethnographic project about collaboration in industry.

Kate Garretson (New York University, Ph.D.) is Coordinator of Professional Development at CUNY's Adult and Continuing Education. She recently completed an ethnographic study of the theoretical practices of three ESL teachers at the college level. She is owner/manager of the electronic bulletin board Slart-l (Second Language Acquisition Research and Teaching).

Gwen Gorzelsky teaches Basic and Critical Writing at the University of Pittsburgh. She has published an article entitled "Riding the Seesaw: Generative Tensions between Teaching Models" in *Resources for Teaching Ways of Reading: An Anthology for Writers,* Ed. David Bartholomae and Anthony Petrosky, 1996.

Carol Peterson Haviland is Assistant Professor of English and Director of the Writing Center as well as Faculty Writing Consultant at California State University, San Bernadino. She has published in *Journal of Basic Writing, College Composition and Communication, English Journal, The Writing Center Journal,* and *Writing Lab Newsletter.* Her research interests are in ethnography, collaboration, writing centers, and writing across the curriculum. She is currently working on a book about interactions between students and tutors in the Writing Center. Her dissertation focused on an interpretative study of how college professors outside English departments talk about practice and teach students about writing.

Cristina Kirklighter teaches first-year and professional writing at the University of South Florida. She has published in *Teaching in the Two Year College, Composition Forum, Text and Performance Quarterly,* and *The Americas Review.* She has also presented papers at CCCCs, MLA, and SAMLA.

Neal Lerner is Writing Center Coordinator and Composition Instructor at the Massachusetts College of Pharmacy & Allied Health Sciences. His most recent publications appear in *Composition Studies* and in two forthcoming collections on writing center research.

John Lofty is an Associate Professor at the University of New Hampshire where he teaches courses in pedagogy: theory and practice of teaching middle- and high-school English and teaching literature at the college level. He is particularly interested in how the social and institutional construction of time influences language learning at the elementary, secondary, and college level. He has published one book on ethnography: *Time to Write: The Influence of Time and Culture on Learning to Write* (SUNY, 1992). He has also published chapters in *College Literature, The Children Speak: Children Talk About Literacy,* and the highly acclaimed book *The Right to Literacy.*

Kay M. Losey is Assistant Professor of English and Assistant Director of the Writing Program at the University of North Carolina at Chapel Hill. Her ethnographic books include *Listen to the Silences: Mexican American Interaction in the Composition Classroom and the Community* (Ablex, 1997) and *Opportunities Lost and Lessons Learned: Inside a Workplace Literacy Program* (with Judy Kalman, *National Center for Research in Vocational Education*, 1992).

Joseph M. Moxley is professor of English at the University of South Florida. Moxley teaches graduate courses in ethnography, research methods, the politics of literacy, and composition theory. He first became interested in ethnography when he completed his dissertation, "Five Writer's Perceptions of Writing Functions, An Ethnographic Study." Since then, he has edited, written, or co-written ten books, including *The Internet Deception*, a novel, and published articles in over thirty journals, such as *College Composition and Communication*.

Keith Rhodes, a former commercial litigation attorney, is currently Asst. Professor and Coordinator of Composition at Northwest Missouri State University. He is interested in alternative publication genres, as indicated by his article "Driving Into the Heart of Henry Giroux's Pedagogy" in *Writing on the Edge*.

Marcy Taylor is Assistant Professor of English at Central Michigan University. She is currently working on the manuscript of a book-length ethnography of adolescent literacy, as well as founding a new English studies journal entitled *Pedagogy: Critical Approaches to Literature, Language and Composition*, along with Jennifer Holberg. She has published a co-authored piece in WPA.

Cloe Vincent teaches courses in rhetoric, composition, professional writing, and Modernist literature. She is currently teaching in the "Writing Across the Curriculum" program at George Mason University. Her primary research interests include the role of the teacher in the writing-intensive classroom, methods for evaluating writing effectively, research methodologies in composition studies, and the use of writing across the disciplines. She has conducted ethnographic research in classroom settings.

Ruoyi Wu is Assistant Professor of English at Stetson University, where she teaches first-year and advanced composition, rhetorical theory, grammar, and autobiography. Her research interests lie in interdisciplinary theories of the self, ESL writers and cross-cultural studies, and ideologies of genres such as autobiography and ethnography.

Kristi Yager teaches at the University of Wisconsin-Milwaukee. Her previous publications include "The Saming Game: Composition and Emotion" (*Writing on the Edge,* Fall 1995) and "Romantic Resonances in Peter Elbow's Writing Without Teachers" (*Composition Studies,* Spring 1996).

Bibliography

Agar, M. 1982. "Toward an Ethnographic Language." *American Anthropologist* 84:779–795.

Althusser, L. 1969. "On the Materialist Dialectic." *For Marx*. Trans. B. Brewster. New York: Pantheon. 163–218.

American Anthropology Association. 1966. Final report of the commission to review the AAA statements on ethics. *Anthropology Newsletter* 37(4):13–15.

American Anthropology Association. 1966. Draft AAA code of ethics. *Anthropology Newsletter* 37(4):15–16.

Aristotle. 1954. *The Rhetoric and Poetics of Aristotle*. Trans. W. R. Roberts. New York: Modern Library.

Athanases, S., and S. B. Heath. 1995. "Ethnography in the Study of the Teaching and Learning of English." *Research in the Teaching of English* 29(3):263–287.

Atkinson, P. 1990. *The Ethnographic Imagination: Textual Constructions of Reality*. London: Routledge.

_____. 1992. *Understanding Ethnographic Texts*. Thousand Oaks, CA: Sage.

Babcock, B. A. 1980. "Reflexivity: Definitions and Discriminations." *Semiotica* 30(1–2):1–14.

Bakhtin, M. 1981. "Discourse in the Novel." In *The Dialogic Imagination*. Trans. C. Emerson and M. Holquist. Ed. M. Holquist. University of Texas Slavic Series 1. Austin: University of Texas Press.

Ball, S. J. 1990. "Self Doubt and Soft Data: Social and Technical Trajectories in Ethnographic Fieldwork." *Qualitative Studies in Education* 3:157–171.

Barnes. J. A. 1977. *The Ethics of Inquiry in Social Sciences*. Delhi: Oxford University Press.

Bartholomae, D. 1988. Review of *The Making of Knowledge in Composition: Portrait of an Emerging Field*. *Rhetoric Review* 6(2):224–228.

_____. 1990. "A Reply to Stephen North." *Pre/Text* 11(1–2):121–130.

Berlin, J. 1987. *Rhetoric and Reality*. Carbondale, IL: Southern Illinois University Press.

Bishop, W. 1990. *Something Old, Something New: College Writing Teachers and Classroom Change*. Studies in Writing and Rhetoric. Carbondale, IL: Southern Illinois University Press.

_____. 1992. "I-Witnessing in Composition: Turning Ethnographic Data into Narratives." *Rhetoric Review* 11(Fall):147–158.

_____. 1994. "The Perils, Pleasures, and Process of Ethnographic Writing Research." In *Taking Stock: Reassessing the Writing Process Movement in the 90s*. Eds. T. Newkirk and L. Tobin. Portsmouth, NH: Boynton/Cook.

————. Forthcoming, Fall 97. *Ethnographic Writing Research: Writing It Down, Writing It Up, and Reading It.* Portsmouth, NH: Boynton/Cook.

Bissex, G. L., and R. H. Bullock. 1987. *Seeing for Ourselves.* Portsmouth, NH: Boynton/Cook.

Bizzell, P. 1994. " 'Contact Zones' and English Studies." *College English* 56:163–169.

Blau, P. 1974. *On the Nature of Organizations.* New York: John Wiley & Sons.

Boas, F. 1973. "Scientists as Spies." In *To See Ourselves.* Ed. Thomas Weaver. Glenview, IL: Scott, Foresman.

Bogdan, R. C., and S. K. Biklen. 1982. *Qualitative Research for Education.* Boston, MA: Allyn and Bacon.

————. 1992. *Qualitative Research in Education: An Introduction to Theory and Methods.* 2d ed. Boston, MA: Allyn and Bacon.

Borgatti, S. P., M. G. Everett, and L. C. Freeman. 1992. *UCINET IV Version 1.6.* Columbia: Analytic Technologies.

Bourdieu, P. 1967. "Systems of Education and Systems of Thought." *International Social Science Journal* 3:338–358.

Brandt, D. 1986. "Toward an Understanding of Context in Composition." *Written Communication* 3:139–157.

Branscomb, H. E. 1995. "Shadows of Doubt: Writing Research and the New Epistemologies." *College English* 57:469–480.

Britzman, D. 1991. *Practice Makes Practice: A Critical Study of Learning to Teach.* Albany: State University of New York Press.

Brodkey, L. 1987a. "Writing Critical Ethnographic Narratives." *Anthropology & Education Quarterly* 18:67—76.

————. 1987b. "Writing Ethnographic Narratives." *Written Communication* 4(1):25–50.

————. 1989. "On the Subjects of Class and Gender in *The Literacy Letters.*" *College English* 51:125–141.

————. 1991. "Tropics of Literacy." In *Rewriting Literacy: Culture and the Discourse of the Other.* Ed. Candace Mitchell and Kathleen Weiler. New York: Bergin and Garvey.

Brodzki, B., and C. Schenck. 1988. *Life/Lines: Theorizing Women's Autobiography.* Ithaca, NY: Cornell University Press.

Brooke, R. 1987. "Underlife and Writing Instruction." *College Composition and Communication* 38(2):141–153.

————. 1991. *Writing and Sense of Self: Identity Negotiating Writing Workshops.* Urbana, IL: National Council of Teachers of English.

Brueggemann, B. J. 1996. "Still Life: Representations and Silences in the Participant–Observer Role." In *Ethics and Representation in Qualitative Studies of Literacy.* Eds. G. Kirsch and P. Mortenson. Urbana, IL: National Council of Teachers of English.

Bruner, J. 1986. *Actual Minds, Possible Worlds.* Cambridge, MA: Harvard University Press.